Report Cards to Paychecks

Get Fired Up Strategies for Succeeding in College and Life

By
Famous Dave Anderson
James W. Anderson

Copyright 2010 by DWA Holdings LLC
Printed in the United States of America

Some books are written to help you survive college.

This book is written to help you SUCCEED in college and in life!

If your ambition is to go to college, you will be shocked to discover...

70% of high school students fail to graduate
"college ready."
~Manhattan Institute for Policy Research

Only 54% of all college students will graduate.
~National Center for Education Statistics

75% of college students lack skills
to perform real-life tasks.
~CNN.com

50% of all college students report feeling so depressed at some points in the last semester that they had trouble functioning. Suicide remains the second leading cause of death of college students.
~The American Psychiatric Association

$27,803 is the student average cumulative debt
for a 4-year undergraduate degree.
~2008 National Post Secondary Student Aid Study
(Students are starting out broke before they even get started in life!)

64% of all workers under the age 25
are unhappy with their jobs.
~TNS Global Market Research

STUDENTS: The Odds of Graduating From College Are Against You. Improve your odds by devouring this book! Mastering these Success Skills will give you an unfair advantage over the millions of other college graduates competing for your job! This amazing book on "How To Succeed In College" is jam packed with proven street smart strategies to achieving the best grades possible and turning your college experience into the best years of your life!

TABLE OF CONTENTS

Introduction..8

Chapter 1: You Were Born to Win....................................... 10

Chapter 2: College Is A Fresh Start 21

Chapter 3: Discovering YOU! 28

Chapter 4: Create Your Own Personal Brand 33

Chapter 5: Discover Your "Compelling Force" That Will
            Drive You Relentlessly Toward Success in
            College.. 42

Chapter 6: Don't Spend One Day In College Without Goals 49

Chapter 7: Visualize Your Goals 63

Chapter 8: Follow Your Dreams and Pursue Your
            Passion.. 67

Chapter 9: The 19 Most Critical Character Traits
            Employers Look for in Graduates 78

Chapter 10: Before You Begin College... Write Out Your
            Resume and Job Recommendations.................... 87

Chapter 11: Your First Day of College is Actually Your
            First Day on the Job!.................................. 92

Chapter 12: Famous Dave's "Inside Secret" to Success............... 96

Chapter 13: The "Leading Edge Difference" That Will
            Have Your Professors Talking You Up All
            Over Campus! 102

Chapter 14: Kick Start Your Career By Interning and
Working as an Apprentice 115

Chapter 15: Powerhouse Networking...................................126

Chapter 16: Don't Expect Success, If You Haven't Studied
Success!...131

Chapter 17: Personal Research and Development and
Understanding "The Four Career Knowledge
Areas" of Intellectual Capital 134

Chapter 18: The Shocking Secret to Success in College,
Your Career, and Life! 141

Chapter 19: Financial Literacy 150

Chapter 20: Great Ideas to Help You Get the Most Out of
Your College Investment 157

Chapter 21: Let's Party... No Thanks I've Got to Go Study! 191

Chapter 22: Final Thoughts 198

INTRODUCTION

Hi! This is Famous Dave Anderson along with my son James Anderson and we are excited that you have chosen to read the best How To Succeed In College book ever written! Yes, this is a very boastful statement, but our real-world success has proven these ideas work. As a successful business owner, I have spent millions of dollars researching and creating the best training programs for our restaurants and I am sharing the best skill-building techniques for this book. Over the years I have read through thousands of resumes of college graduates and know firsthand what it takes to make a great hire.

Throughout my business career, many of my Famous Dave's customers have commented that I must have been blessed, because it seems like everything I touch turns to gold. I surprise these folks when I share with them that my success has been fueled by tremendous adversity, failure including bankruptcy, and personal tragedy. Then, they really want to know how I was able to achieve success in my life and if there are any special insights that I can share to help them or their sons and daughters. I have shared my street-smart strategies to millions across the US including Canada and now for the first time I am sharing my strategies for College Success! The strategies in this book work, as I am living proof. I went from being in the bottom half of my high school class with no undergraduate degree to a Master's Degree from Harvard University. And today, Presidents of Universities ask me to come speak to their students! I figured it is now time to share all my learning secrets with everyone.

My son James worked side-by-side with me in the early days building Famous Dave's into one of the hottest restaurant concepts in America! James also has over 10 successful years in the personal development field as a speaker, author, and trainer, and has trained over 2,000 top executives and college students. James has collaborated with me on this book to identify the best success skills needed to achieve academic excellence in college, while building a solid foundation for succeeding in the real-world.

Our goal is to inspire all students to achieve the best grades possible while having the greatest time of their college life! Our advice to college students is that the "real-world" does not start after college, the "real-world" starts... NOW! Your first day in college is really your first day on the job. Our mission is to turn academic report cards into real-world paychecks.

We Believe Our Higher Purpose in Life is to make a positive difference in the lives of others by giving them hope. Life is tough and full of adversity. We believe that no matter how tough things may be... if you never give up on yourself, never give up on your dreams, and are willing to work hard... you will always overcome adversities to success and be able to enjoy the unlimited rewards of your wildest dreams!

Your college diploma won't mean a thing if you don't graduate with the following documents and strategies for living a successful life!

1. A written down list of your 100 greatest dreams
2. A written down list of your goals
3. A Vision Book
4. Creating your Personal Brand
5. Discovering your life's true passion
6. A yearly Financial Plan and Budget
7. 30 second Elevator Speech about yourself
8. A powerful introduction that will open all doors
9. A resume that will have every employer lined up at our door
10. Job recommendations that will set you up for life!

Read this book actively. Work on every idea, strategy, and success skill. If you leave with college with the above 10 things completed as much as you can, you will be in the top 3% of the achievers in the world!

CHAPTER ONE

You Were Born to Win

You Don't Need the Best Grades to Succeed in Life!
The most important character traits for anyone's success are the *drive* and *determination* to achieve their dreams. All successful people have incredible visions for their lives and they won't let anything stop them until they succeed. Now, having said this... you owe it to yourself to strive for the best grades possible, if for no other reason than to prove to yourself that you can master any intellectual discipline you set out to learn!

If you have topnotch, good grades, that's great! You're ahead of the game. Let's face it: Some kids are amazingly bright and some people, like me, just have to work harder. All my life, I have struggled to learn stuff, but I persisted until I became a huge success. I share these stories of my own academic hardships because if I could succeed, both academically and in my career, then I am living proof that anything is possible.

For most of my years in high school, I sincerely thought that I was the dumbest kid the in class and my grades were proof. My parents used to make me sit at the kitchen table every night trying to get me to study, but I couldn't keep my mind on what I was doing. My dad used to yell at me for getting bad grades, and soon I hated school. In class, I would look around at my classmates and wonder why they were so smart and I was so dumb. I was the kid in the bottom half of the class that made the top half possible!

Famous Dave's Key Lesson: *"No one can keep you from accomplishing your dreams!"* Pursue your dreams with a fierce passion, believing you are unstoppable and you will achieve phenomenal success. That is the real message of this book.

I Used to Think There Was No Hope for Me, Until I Found Out... *I Was Born To Win!*

There came a point in high school when I became awakened or enlightened to the fact: *I was never going to be the brightest kid in class and I was never going to be the most talented.* There was no use fooling myself thinking anything else was possible. For many years, that scared me—until I had the very fortunate opportunity to hear motivational speaker Zig Ziglar say, "You were born to win!"

Anything is Possible!

WOW! I had never heard anyone ever tell me that I was "born to win." And from that day on I started a lifelong journey to discover what I was actually capable of achieving. Today, I have learned that success is all about a person's attitude and willingness to work. If you have an attitude that *you hope* to become a success, you'll never achieve it. But if you have a deep, unwavering belief that you are going to succeed and you are willing to work nonstop until you have achieved your dreams, then I sincerely believe you will succeed beyond your wildest dreams!

I am a believer that it doesn't matter where you come from or what you've been through. The only thing that matters is that, in this great country, if you have a dream and you are willing to work hard, anything is really possible!

> *Nothing will take away persistence. Talent will not; nothing is more common than an unsuccessful man with talent. Genius will not; unrewarded genius is almost a proverb. Education will not; the world is full of educated derelicts. Persistence and determination alone are omnipotent.*
>
> ~Calvin Coolidge
> 30th President of the United States

I Am Relentless to Keep Improving Myself

I work consistently longer and harder than most people. It takes me longer to learn things, but very few people study with the fierce determination I do every single day of my life. I will out-study, make sacrifices, and outwork everyone else. I regularly work 12 to 14 hour days and weekends. It's even rarer that I take vacations. I am fortunate that I love what I do for a living and I have a wife and family who are supportive. I am not advocating my lifestyle, but that is how I have been able to overcome my learning disabilities and all my terrible screw-ups!

If you have God-given talents and you are smart, *you need to be grateful!* But you also need to be relentless in your pursuit of excellence. Cultivate a relentless determination to be the best in your profession. Just having a diploma is not a guarantee for success in this highly competitive marketplace that is rapidly changing, faster then we can sometimes comprehend. Every day when you wake up, make "RELENTLESS: driven with unwavering determination" one of your personal trademarks.

Famous Dave's Key Lesson: While you are young, physically able, and mentally alert, this is when you want to work harder, longer hours, and push yourself to create a solid foundation for building a very successful career. Start developing a solid reputation for having a great work ethic. Don't harbor bad thoughts towards studying or work. Discipline yourself to doing homework every day, because you will be doing homework the rest of your life. Create a mindset that you love working. You should love work as much as playing!

> *Success is not the result of spontaneous combustion.*
> *You must set yourself on fire!*
> ~Robin Leach
> Host of *Lifestyles of the Rich and Famous*

SUCCESS SKILLS 101: ATTITUDE IS EVERYTHING!
Success begins with a Positive Attitude, unwavering confidence in yourself, and an optimistic belief that you will persevere through life's toughest challenges. You will succeed. *You will achieve all your greatest dreams. Believe It! Never Doubt It! BELIEVE IT!*

Why You Need to Master the Life Skills in This Book...

YOU WILL BE WHACKED AND JACKHAMMERED BY PROBLEMS AND ADVERSITIES THROUGHOUT LIFE!

You may be wondering, *Why should I read this book?* And you're probably saying to yourself, *I don't have learning disabilities like Famous Dave and I am pretty smart.* I have openly shared these negative things about myself to prove that "just being smart and getting good grades" isn't a sure guarantee for success in life. I have discovered, the hard way, critical life skills that helped me overcome incredible odds and adversities to achieve remarkable success in life, and it's for this purpose that you need to devour and master the success principles found in this book!

One of the Great Lessons in Life: Turn Your Weaknesses Into Your Strengths and Your Worst Adversities Into Your Greatest Opportunities!

This is the stuff you should be learning in college! The most important lesson that I learned for myself is how to always turn my weaknesses into my strengths. How to overcome life's adversities is probably one of the greatest skills you will have to learn the hard way. The important lesson is you can never give up on yourself or your dreams. Despite my learning disabilities, I have excelled in many other areas besides grades.

Some students get the highest grades possible but they have to work for other people because they lack poor social skills or they believe, falsely, that they don't have a creative bone in their bodies. They have become warehouses for facts. This is not the purpose of college. The real purpose of education is not getting you to regurgitate stored-up facts and definitions, but encouraging you to think, make sound decisions, and learn how to get things done. It's always about producing results no matter what you are faced with in life. Learn how to turn negatives into positives. Learn how to turn the impossible into the possible. Turn your weaknesses into your strengths and your worst adversities into your greatest opportunities!

The Secret to My Success May Shock You!

Famous Dave's Key Lesson: For unlimited success... look for PROBLEMS!!! Like many other successful leaders, entrepreneurs, athletes, community activists, politicians, and yes, even parents, I owe my success to my ability to handle problems and to find solutions to problems. Dealing with problems is life's great secret to uncommon success. No one has ever said, "Let's get Dave Anderson on our team because this guy went to Harvard and he got good grades in school." Everyone says, "We need Dave Anderson on our team because this guy is good at overcoming problems. Dave knows how to find solutions. He doesn't wilt under pressure! While others whine and complain, Dave is optimistic, always looking for solutions. Dave gets things done!"

I did not learn how to deal with gut-wrenching adversities and hair-pulling problems in school. I learned how to deal with life's toughest challenges from living life. The purpose of this book is to prepare you so that you, too, can successfully take on life's challenges and adversities, and never be scared by stepping up when others have disappeared when faced with adversities.

> *Life's challenges are not supposed to paralyze you, they're supposed to help you discover who you are!*
> ~Dr. Bernice Johnson Reagon
> Great African-American Scholar, Teacher, and Civil Rights Activist

Your Mind is Infinite! Infinite! Infinite! Infinite! Infinite!

The primary goal of education is to awaken you to how incredibly brilliant you are! Education is designed to alert you to the things you need to discover; to process information to innovate new ideas; to form opinions; to create solutions to problems; and to teach you how to influence others about your dreams, aspirations, and ideas. Start believing that your mind is infinite. You have talents waiting to be unleashed. There is nothing you can't accomplish. You were designed for greatness. Ultimately, the real purpose of education is to teach you how to unleash your talents, skills, and giftedness to make the world a better place... and not just to get a job!

There's More to College Than Just Good Grades—Learn Success Skills That Will Help You Achieve in Life!

Achieving the best grades possible is important, but it is also important for you to develop *Success Skills* in the following areas:

- *Social Skills* to be a contributing member of your business or community.
- *Relationship Skills,* as all success begins by cultivating great contacts and resources through a strong network of relationships.
- *Networking Skills,* that allow you to harvest the resources of the incredible people you will meet.
- *Problem Solving Skills,* as all your greatest opportunities will come from solving problems for people to make them delightfully happy!
- *Creative Skills* to come up with new ideas and innovations.
- *Inspirational Skills,* most important of all, to enable you to get get big, Big, BIG RESULTS through *inspiring and influencing people.*

Success Begins By Cultivating Great Relationships: YOU Need To Learn How to Play Nice in the Sandbox!

There's no point to holing up in your dorm room and becoming a recluse while you get straight A's—but then you can't get hired because you have no social skills. Employers want to hire bright, intelligent, passionate, fun-loving people that can best represent their companies. They look to hire people that their clients would enjoy being around. Your employers will question if they can trust you with their best clients or if you can entertain their clients in social settings. It's important that you get a well-rounded college experience that helps you succeed in all areas of your life. The ability to play in college is just as important as studying! So start smiling and saying "Hi!" to everyone you meet.

You can make more friends in two months by becoming really interested in other people than you can in two years by trying to get other people interested in you.
~Dale Carnegie
American Author, Speaker, and Personal-Development Pioneer

I Didn't Get Into HARVARD Because of Good Grades!

David W. Anderson, MPA, PhD. Who knew? As a result of my newfound love for learning—despite having C's, D's, and F's in high school and not having an undergraduate degree—I now have a Master's Degree from Harvard University. It was my life's work, getting involved in helping my community, and my will, perseverance, and determination that opened the doors to Harvard University. And recently, another college presented me with a doctoral for my life's work. Back in high school, my teachers never would have given me more than a snowball's chance in hell that it was possible for me to be a Harvard University graduate.

Don't Misunderstand Me—I Am a Strong Advocate for Education and Lifelong Learning

Today, I am on a "Rampage of Learning." I eat books for breakfast! I will not get into my car unless I have audio books to listen to while I drive. I can't even eat unless I am reading something. In fact, I can't even sit on the family throne unless I have a book to read! I have learned that I am actually brilliant and one of the nation's most creative people in the restaurant business. I learned that I just have to work harder and study longer hours than everyone else. My life's story proves anything is possible! My story of overcoming incredible odds, personal failures—alcoholism and bankruptcy—and other tough adversities shows how important it is to have an optimistic attitude and to never quit on yourself.

Learn These 3 Secrets to a Successful Life

If you take away anything from this book, just remember that there are three basic rules for success:

1. Always give more than what you are paid.
2. It's not about *you* but about your obsessively devoted service to make other people happy and their lives better.
3. You will always succeed if all you do is outwork everyone else and then turn around and help those around you to become more productive and successful as well.

Setting the World On Fire and Making It Famous!
Today, I have created several publicly traded companies on Wall Street. I have created billions in revenues. I have created over 20,000 new jobs. And Famous Dave's of America, Inc, the World's Greatest Rib Joint, has been recognized as one of the "Hottest Restaurant Concepts in America"! I am living proof that you don't need the best grades in school to succeed—but you do need *drive and determination* to follow your passion, a willingness to work hard, and an unwavering mindset to never ever give up on yourself. If you keep this unstoppable mindset, then anything you set your mind to achieving...becomes possible! If you have good grades and a diploma, you're ahead of the game—but you will still be held responsible for creating *above-average results*. "Just getting by" doesn't cut it anymore. The marketplace does not reward "average." You are NOT going to college just to be "average!"

My Success Proves the Ideas and Strategies in This Book Will Work, So Use This Book Daily!
You will achieve greater results if you use this book as an *active study guide* until you master these ideas and make them an integral part of your daily life. Mastery of the Life Skills and Success Skills detailed in this book should be your daily driving ambition.

> *Getting ahead in a difficult profession requires avid faith in yourself. That is why some people with mediocre talent, but with great inner drive, go much further than people with vastly superior talent.*
> ~Sophia Loren
> Academy Award-Winning Actress

SUCCESS SKILLS 101:Pursue Your Passion
Follow your dreams. Spend your life doing the one thing you love. Don't spend a lifetime doing something you don't love to do. Your passion should consume you. When you love something so much, your desire will drive you to become the best at this one thing. You will want to make others delightfully happy with your service or the product of your passion. When this happens, the marketplace will find you and pay you... beyond your wildest expectations!

My Thoughts On Going to College "Just To Get A Job"

Many students, when asked why they are going to college, reply, "I need a degree so I can get a good-paying job." DON'T go to college just to get a job! If you learn anything, know the difference between a JOB, which is an acronym for Just Over Broke, and an *opportunity*. This is also the same for the difference between "being employed" and "being employable." Or for someone saying they "have to go to work to earn a living." How about going to work to "create a life worth living"?! Learning *success skills to create value* and not just book knowledge should be your goal in college. Learning *how to create value* will help you achieve your greatest potential throughout your career. Master the skills outlined in this book and you will always be in demand.

> *Earning your degree should not be your only goal. because the knowledge you stuff your head with about Business, Chemistry, Medicine, Technology or any other college major is almost obsolete the day you graduate. In the new, rapidly changing world of today, "How to thrive successfully in any environment and how to stay technically updated and relevant" should be the knowledge you seek in your college studies. But the best advice I can share is to master, "How to be exceptional in obsessive devoted service to others!" If you can better the lives of others by creating value beyond expectation, you will always be in demand in the marketplace. Then ask yourself: Is this what I am learning in my classes?*
> ~Famous Dave Anderson
> Founder of the World's Greatest BBQ Joint

Famous Dave's Key Lesson: Understand the huge difference between "getting a job" and "always being employable." Don't make getting a job your goal for college... make "always being employable" your goal. Strive to get the best grades possible with the same intensity as you would working on your first job. How you study in college will be a good indicator to how you will commit to being excellent at your first job.

THE NEW REALITY... DON'T SKIP THIS PAGE!!!!

Job Security and Retirement Are Dead Concepts!

Today, job security is an obscure, dead concept, just like retirement is a dead concept of the industrial age! Today's graduate is now competing for jobs against a global job pool. Some of the brightest, most hardworking, multi-language graduates are coming from India and China. High-paying American jobs are now easily outsourced to countries where highly skilled workers are willing to work for $1 an hour. Even high-paying jobs in technology, engineering, accounting, and law that demand hourly fees of $500 an hour in America, can be outsourced to highly skilled professionals in other countries for $25 an hour!

Graduates, here's something scary to think about...

Did you know that 25 percent of the students in India are on the Honor Roll? But here's the real point: Those 25 percent of students on the Honor Roll in India are more people than *all* of the students in the United States! And guess what? They are all striving to get jobs in United States. So, how are you going to compete against so many talented people who are willing to work longer and harder hours for less money?

Retirement May Not Be an Option Today

Today, one new innovative product can wipe out an entire industry overnight. Companies are laying off workers by the tens of thousands; and, unlike the old days, these companies are not hiring them back. Don't just learn job skills; learn skills that will help you to always be in a position of "creating value for others."

Your value to the marketplace will never be based on your job skills, but on how successful you are in making others happy! Master the skills in this book and you will never have to fear standing in the unemployment line waiting for a handout from the government.

Today, the average college graduate will have three to five career changes and 10 to 14 job changes by the age of 38.
~U.S. Department of Labor

COLLEGE SUCCESS TIPS: The Real Stuff You Should Be Learning in College!

1. No one can keep you from accomplishing your dreams! Claim your dreams and burn them into your heart and mind. Cultivate a *relentless drive* with *unwavering determination* to make all your dreams and goals come true. Create a mindset that you are unstoppable!
2. *You are 100 percent responsible for everything that happens in your life. There are no excuses.* You cannot blame others. It's your choices that determine your action and behavior and the results. You are always responsible for the results of whatever happens in your life.
3. Remind yourself throughout the day that you have *the seeds of greatness within you! You were Born To Win!*
4. All success begins with a positive attitude, unwavering confidence in yourself, and an optimistic belief that will compel you to persevere through all of life's challenges.
5. Learn to turn your weaknesses into your strengths and your adversities into your opportunities.
6. Nothing is impossible. Anything is possible. Believe it! Embrace it! Just do it!
7. Your success will depend on your ability to cultivate great relationships. Get to know someone new every day. Get into the habit of writing down as much information on these new people so you will always remember them. Then stay in touch!
8. The greatest rewards in life will be discovered when you learn how to solve other people's problems and make their lives enjoyable! Remember: It's not about you!
9. Be a giver, not a taker. Give beyond expectation. Give more than you are paid—this is called "creating value." Creating value, making others happy, and turning adversities into opportunities will create unlimited rewards beyond your wildest dreams!
10. Learn the difference between being employed and being employable. The difference between getting a job and creating opportunity. And finally, learn the difference between earning a living and creating a life worth living!

CHAPTER TWO

College is a Fresh Start

"The Future's So Bright, I Gotta Wear Shades!"
~Timbuk 3
American Alternative Band, 1980's Hit Song Title

Spread Your Wings and Soar! You're Independent! Free to Do Your Own Thing!

College: The Best Years of Your Life!
The greatest change you will immediately notice about going to college is that you are now on your own. No bossy parents telling you when to go to bed, what to eat, or to do your homework. You are on your own. This can either be your biggest opportunity or it can be the beginning of your biggest downfall.

College Is a Fresh Start
No matter what happened in high school, you now have the opportunity to reinvent yourself! Yes, you are now free to make your own decisions; but, hopefully, you will be responsible and show your maturity to think things through. Going to college allows you to spread your wings, to be adventurous, and to explore what you are really capable of achieving on your own.

Learn to overcome all your fears. Fear only exists in your mind. Don't spend the most wonderful years of your life holed up in a college dorm room. Make new friends. Attend on-campus debates and concerts, and support your school's sports teams. Take part in student government. Find a way to express your ideas, dreams, and aspirations. Check out all student activities. Break out of your shyness and say "Hi!" to a stranger!

Have Fun—But Don't Go Off the Deep End!

Just because you have freedom doesn't mean you can be loose as a goose doing whatever you please! Yes, there is the thrill of partying and drinking without your parents around. You are now old enough to entertain yourself however you want. But is this what college really means to you?

> *There are only two lasting gifts we can hope to give our children. One of these is roots, the other, wings.*
> ~Hodding Carter
> Pulitzer Prize-Winning Author

College Is Your Opportunity to Prove to the World...
You've Arrived!

Hopefully, you will see your independence as your opportunity to prove you are mature and can make responsible decisions as an adult and not as some wild teen who doesn't have parents around. This is an unbelievable opportunity for you to prove that you are amazing—not how totally weird you can be just to prove to your parents that they can't tell you what to do anymore.

Life's Greatest Opportunities Will Come From Your Greatest Sacrifices in the Next Four Years!

Many adults living frustrated lives wish they had their college years back so they could put more effort into their studies. The more you give up to stay the course until graduation, the more you will reveal your true desire to achieve all your greatest dreams in life. Your willingness to sacrifice your youthful impulsive indulgences so you can invest your time and energy into making the most out of your education will set the foundation for a successful career and a very rewarding life.

> *If you think education is expensive,*
> *you should try ignorance!*
> ~Derek Bok
> President, Harvard University, 1971-1991

The Following Short Lists Are Thoughts and Ideas You Should Think About to Get the Most Out of Your College Experience

The 3 Most Important Things You Must Get Out of Your College Experience—More Important Than Just Grades:

1. **A Diploma.** You must graduate and get your diploma, proving to the world that you have the discipline to think, research, innovate, create, get results, and follow something through until completion.
2. **Learning How to be Independent.** Learn how to take care of yourself and be responsible for living on your own.
3. **Great Job Recommendations.** Learn the secrets of getting great recommendations from your professors for the job of your dreams! Being able to get referrals or testimonials will be a valuable Success Skill you will use the rest of your career.

The 3 Terrific Ideas That Will Dramatically Transform Your College Experience into a Successful Career:

1. **Your career begins on your first day at college**...not when you get a job.
2. **Think of college as your job.** It will change how you show up for class! Treat professors and school officials as your bosses. Getting comfortable with people in authority will help you with your bosses in the real world. Treat all your classmates as your potential most valued customers or employees. This will help you build great relationship skills and learn never to burn bridges. Thinking of a fellow classmate as a future customer or employer will encourage you to treat EVERY student with respect and cheerfulness.
3. **It's Not About You!** Take what you are learning not for your own personal gain or edification, but instead figure out how to use your education to "Create Value" for the purpose of bettering the lives of other people. This is education's greatest untold secret for unlimited opportunity!

The 3 Valuable Character Traits You Must Master in College to Help You Succeed in Life:

1. **An Optimistic Attitude.** Cultivate an upbeat, positive spirit so strong that nothing will ever defeat your optimistic, forward-looking outlook on life. Sparkle with enthusiasm! (Don't worry about what others may think about your cheerfulness and optimism. You will stand out in this negative world!)
2. **An Unstoppable Drive.** Cultivate a personal drive of being a self-starter. Be someone who makes things happen. Take initiative. Be industrious.
3. **Unwavering Determination.** Cultivate an internal, undefeatable, persistent, and relentless drive that will never quit until you reach your goals and you have realized your greatest dreams.

God has blessed you with an amazing mind and incredible talent. Failure to work diligently to discover what you are capable of achieving is a tragedy against yourself and all of mankind.

~James W. Anderson
Entrepreneur, Speaker, and Author

The 3 Transformational Ideas You Should Embrace:

1. **I am 100 percent responsible for whatever happens in my life!** Take full responsibility. Make no excuses and NEVER be blameful.
2. **You are amazing and there are *no limits to what YOU can accomplish!*** You have everything within you, right now, to succeed and achieve all of your greatest dreams and goals.
3. **It's not about you—it's all about serving others.** Live a life of service to others and they will help you achieve all your wildest dreams!

Nobody can go back and start a new beginning, but anyone can start today and make a new ending.

~Maria Robinson
American Writer and Student of Life

YOU ARE RESPONSIBLE!

Once you turn 18, you are 100 percent responsible for whatever happens in your life. There are no excuses. What happens in life is like playing cards. You are dealt a hand of cards, and you can't change the cards you were dealt. However, your choice or your decisions decide how you are going to play your hand. How you play your hand is 100 percent up to you. Give everything a full out 100 percent over-the-top effort. Be the best you can be at everything you do. Be the one everyone counts on. You can make a difference. Make the world a better place Remember: *If it's to be, it's up to ME!* You are the future of the world!

> *There are three types of men. The one that learns by reading, the few who learn by observation, the rest of them have to pee on the electric fence for themselves!*
> ~Will Rogers
> Cherokee Indian, Cowboy, Famous Actor, Comedian, Author

SUCCESS SKILLS 101: Don't Fear Change

Look for positive ways to transform yourself completely into something greater. The hardest lesson to grasp is that you cannot achieve your greatest dreams being the person you are now. Challenge yourself to change, reinvent yourself every year, and don't get stuck in a rut being "the same you" every year. Break out of your comfort zone; do something you have been afraid to do but always wanted to try. Don't get too comfortable with your old friends—you won't grow. Never fear establishing new relationships with exciting, successful, and challenging people who live to break down barriers that seem impossible. Strive to take yourself to higher levels of success and achievement! Never fear change again! Be curious! Discover all that life has to offer—but, more importantly, discover what you are capable of achieving. You are *amazing!* You are *incredible!* Your mind is *infinite! You are the future!*

COLLEGE SUCCESS TIPS: 12 KEY LESSONS

1. Get rid of any self-limiting beliefs you've had in the past. College is a fresh start. This is your first real opportunity to be responsible, make decisions, take chances, and even fail miserably. College is your opportunity to discover your true potential. Whatever you discover, you are actually capable of achieving ten times that!

2. Get out of your comfort zone. Don't work on re-creating your old comfort zones in college. In life, there is no opportunity in security. Meet new people. Create new friendships. Try new things. Get involved. Test yourself. See what you can do. Be curious! Explore! Discover!

3. Learn to get things done when they need to be done with a positive attitude. Do everything to the best of your ability with excellence. Success in college is all about cultivating personal discipline to produce above-average results consistently.

4. College is what YOU make of it! If college is boring to you, it's because you are boring. Just like in life, those who find their jobs boring are actually boring people themselves! Learn how to brighten up every room you walk into!

5. Learn how to research and find *significant* information that changes lives. Learn how to organize your information to create compelling ideas and purposeful statements that are convincing. Knowledge will help you become a person of contribution and influence.

6. You must prepare yourself in college to stand up and stand out competitively against all the other eager young people fighting to take your job. Learn how to stoke yourself up into a competitive firestorm of opportunity!

7. Learn and practice team spirit. Get involved and contribute. Become the person everyone wants on their team. Be a contributing team member who helps the team win or achieve its goal. In the real world, these skills will be invaluable in helping your company compete successfully against the competitors trying to crush you out of existence!

8. College gives you the opportunity to practice financial and fiduciary responsibility. College is the first time you are responsible for balancing your own budget. How you manage your college finances will be a direct reflection on your ability to be responsible with your employer's assets. *Whether you work for a business or a non-profit... it's always about the numbers!*

9. Probably one of the most helpful lessons you will learn will be developing your social skills "to play nice in the sand box." Employers look for outgoing graduates who can meet and entertain clients and who will be great at promoting their company and their products.

10. Don't kid yourself about why you are in college. It's about the money and being the best to beat out your competitors! It's also about developing success skills to help your teammates grow so you can all work together to beat out your competitors.

11. Going to college is not just about getting a job. You can get a job now and you can work your way up the success ladder if all you do is show up and work hard. Your ambition for getting a college degree is to give yourself the best competitive advantage over everyone else, to become the absolute best that you can be, and to make the big bucks sooner while making the world a better place!

12. No matter what job you are studying for, it's all about putting money into the bank. Never forget this. Whether you are a doctor, professor, lawyer, preacher, or politician, you have to know how your job puts money into the bank. Don't fool yourself into believing that you are going to college for any other purpose... It's all about putting money into the bank!

The masses live their lives in quiet frustration believing they either missed or never got a chance at opportunity. The successful create their own opportunities. Once you create your own opportunities, an amazing thing happens—opportunities start to search you out!
~Famous Dave Anderson
Founder of the World's Greatest BBQ Joint!

CHAPTER THREE

Discovering YOU!

You Are Amazing!

The greatest discovery you'll ever make... is not what you will discover studying academic disciplines in school. The most amazing discovery will be the discovery of the incredible untapped potential that is within you, just waiting to be unleashed!

> *More gold has been mined from the thoughts of men than has been taken from the earth.*
>
> ~Napoleon Hill
> Legendary Author of the Amazing Book *Think and Grow Rich*

Don't Be Your Own Critic

Squash any self-limiting beliefs you may have about not being worthy of achieving unlimited success. It's common for kids in college to question their value to society and whether they will successfully compete against all the other bright kids in the world. The most destructive things that rob college kids of their dreams are stress and a feeling they are not deserving—or that somehow they are not smart enough in comparison to their classmates. Don't ever beat yourself down. Give yourself a chance! Before anyone can ever believe in you, you must first believe in yourself! You are more incredible than you think! You are amazingly smart! The universe has given you reasons and a purpose for being alive!

> *What lies behind us and what lies before us are small matters compared to what lies within us!*
>
> ~Ralph Waldo Emerson
> One of America's Most Influential Authors

Cultivate a Healthy, Optimistic Outlook on Life

Believe in yourself. Believe in your dreams. Keep a positive, healthy, optimistic attitude about your future and believe that you are going to set the world on fire and make the world a better place. Create a positive, successful self-image of yourself and burn this vision into every cell of your body. Don't ever let anybody rob you of the vision you have of yourself. I have found that the most important thing in life is to believe in yourself and your dreams. If you are willing to work hard and give more than is expected of you... you will succeed. That's what matters most.

Everyone Wants You to Succeed!

Starting out in college, you may feel like you're all alone against the big, vast world. Take comfort in knowing that everyone at college wants you to succeed. The school would not have given you acceptance if they didn't think you had what it takes to set the world ablaze! Start with the belief that everyone in the whole school are your biggest fans and they are all cheering for you to succeed. Your professors, your advisors, and your entire college—they all want you to succeed. Your responsibility is simple: Get out of your comfort zone to go meet your professors and your advisors. Get help from a tutor if you need it. The most important thing is to be comfortable seeking help when you need it, not after it's too late! Make sure you know and understand all the resources your college has to offer, and don't be afraid to make use of these services—you are paying for them!

> *Men often become what they believe themselves to be. If I believe I cannot do something, it makes me incapable of doing it. But when I believe I can, then I acquire the ability to do it even if I didn't have it in the beginning.*
> ~Mahatma Gandhi
> World's Most Influential Human Rights Activist

It's Not the Grades, But Rather *Your Self-discipline and Determination* to Get the Good Grades, That Really Matters

The most important strategy you will learn about getting good grades is not "the getting" of the good grades but rather developing *the discipline* it takes to get the good grades. Students often complain about why they have to take so many really dumb courses that they will never use in life. Here's the answer: The key to learning is not in the coursework but the discipline it takes day in and day out to do things you don't like to do and yet excel at these things. Next is doing your work with an optimistic and cheerful attitude. Then comes the determination that you will not quit on yourself. Being self-disciplined, having unwavering determination with an optimistic attitude, is basically the definition of success. Doing the things that need to be done, when they need to be done, consistently day in and day out, and always with the same level of consistency and excellence, is the hallmark of people who succeed in life.

Make Discipline Your Friend

Embrace self-discipline and you will accomplish much in life. Make "I'll do whatever I damn please" your motto and it's almost certain you will live a life of failure, frustration, and poverty. There are rules in the game of life. Discipline yourself to become the *Master of the Rules* to turbo-charge your success!

Many times it isn't whether you understand why you are doing something so much as it is that people are counting on you. When you do everything with an all-out effort to produce excellent results, regardless of whether you understand why, you are developing your reputation for doing a job well done and becoming somebody who is trustworthy and reliable.

Personal Discipline Unleashes Your Potential!

It's not the size of the dream that separates the successful from the unsuccessful; it's the size of their desire and the size of their discipline. Most people go through life thinking discipline is something punishing. Discipline actually frees you! Discipline refines your thinking, controls your impulses, and keeps you focused.

Don't Compare Yourself or Be Judgmental of Yourself!

The most important thing you can do for yourself in college is not to compare yourself to the other students. Don't prejudge a lifetime of incredible opportunity by a few years in college. Even more importantly, don't judge your career by your grades. Yes, you absolutely want to get the best grades you can; but it's not always the grades that will determine your success in life. Your belief in yourself, your drive and determination, are often more important than anything else. Always, ALWAYS believe in YOURSELF!

> *If you can find a path with no obstacles, it probably doesn't lead anywhere!*
>
> ~Frank A. Clark
> An Influential Newspaper Cartoonist

Famous Dave's Key Lesson: The greater your discipline, the greater your dreams can be. Discipline is rocket fuel for your goals. *Can you imagine what you could accomplish if your discipline was as great as your dreams?*

SUCCESS SKILLS 101: Successful People Have Favorite Affirmations They Repeat Over and Over to Themselves

One of the keys to being a person of great discipline is programming your mind with positive affirmations that will help you keep focused on your goals. Your mind needs to be primed with positive affirmations to start the day. Throughout the day, after being bombarded by all the negativity in the world, recharge or re-energize your mind with pure, clean, powerful thoughts. Here are my favorites. When confronted by obstacles: *"There's always a way!"* Adversities: *"This too shall pass!"* and *"The Best Is Yet To Come!"* Thoughts on quitting: *"You can't stop a man who won't quit!"* Tough challenges: *"I do what others will not do!"* and *"Every day in every way I get better and better!"* Opportunity: *"If it's to be, it's up to me!"* I will say these affirmations to myself a hundred times throughout the day! I will refuse to let negatives get me down; instead, I will fill my thoughts with positive, uplifting affirmations!

COLLEGE SUCCESS TIPS: Discover What's Within You Already and Waiting to Be Unleashed!

1. You are amazing! Before anyone can believe in you, you must first believe in yourself.
2. Squash all self-limiting beliefs about yourself. Don't ever put yourself down. Be confident. You have unlimited potential that is just waiting to be unleashed!
3. Start cultivating an optimistic outlook on life. Your ATTITUDE has everything to do with your success. Don't ever hesitate. Be a go-getter! Make it happen!
4. Self-discipline unleashes your potential. Make discipline your friend.
5. Create a list of positive affirmations to repeat to yourself throughout your day. Constant reinforcement of your mind will help you stay focused, achieve your goals, and stay optimistic even during tough times.

CHAPTER FOUR

Create Your Personal Brand

Your Personal Brand Called...YOU, Inc.
When you enter college, they may give you a student ID number, which will be forgotten soon after you graduate. However, the "Personal Brand" you are creating every day—called YOU, Inc.—will be remembered forever. You know you've reached the summit when people *instantly* know you by your first name, like Tiger, Oprah, or Elvis. A brand's value is in how fast is "instant" recognition! Or if stamping the name on a product causes the product to be perceived as having become more marketable and valuable.

A brand can represent many things. With people like Oprah, Elvis, or Tiger, their brand name represents professionalism, excellence, market dominance, proven success, credibility, and trust. In products, a brand name like Kleenex, Band Aids, Coke, Lexus, and Bose can represent quality, price, reliability, and market dominance. Even Iron Man, Sponge Bob, and Batman are brands with their own identities, language, dress, and behavior recognition. We live in a world driven by brand names

The most successful brands have developed cult-like status such as that of Harley Davidson. Harley's lifelong, raving, loyal ambassadors practically worship this legendary motorcycle. Devotees wear Harley underwear, socks, belts, jackets, T-shirts, and caps. They eat and drink out of Harley dishes. They sport Harley tattoos on all parts of their bodies and they name their kids Harley while dressing them in Harley pajamas. Today, Harley Davidson has evolved from just being a product into becoming a *lifestyle*.

> ## SUCCESS SKILLS 101: The Brand Called YOU, Inc.
> The value of knowledge is to make a positive difference in the lives of others. Your effectiveness becomes your brand. Don't take the development of your brand image casually. Decide how you want to be remembered. Your personal brand is immediately established by your preceding reputation, first impressions, speech, appearance, and body language. The brand called YOU, Inc. is reinforced over time by your attitude, behavior, and the relationships you create. The most successful Personal Branding occurs when *instant* recognition happens as soon as somebody says your name. How do you want to be remembered?

Your College Years Start Building the Foundation for How You Will Be Remembered for Life

Your name, reputation, achievements, or failures create a personal brand that represents your character, work ethic, and value to the marketplace. A college is known by the quality of the students it graduates. For example, "a Harvard graduate" means something; "a West Point graduate" means something. A successful business or organization is known by the quality of employees it attracts. Your value to the marketplace will largely depend upon your reputation or the recognition of your personal brand. Your personal brand, like the first impression you make when someone meets you, is hard to change once it gets established. You want to pay attention to how you are creating your personal brand and you want to protect your personal brand in the same way you protect your good name and reputation. (Watch what goes on your Facebook page, including what your friends are posting to your wall!)

How You Are Remembered in the Classroom Will Determine the Quality of Your Job Recommendations and References

In college, your grades, relationships with faculty, campus involvement, and team spirit all play into consideration in your ability to get hired. If a recruiter were to call one of your professors, would the professor sound puzzled as they tried to remember you, or would they instantly light up with joy as they recall the great lasting impression you made in their class?

To Stand Up and Stand Out Doesn't Mean Being Weird!

Unfortunately, some students feel that to separate themselves from all the rest of the students they have to be over-the-top "different." I would like to propose that while college is a great opportunity for you to spread your wings and have fun, you should also seriously consider that you are building your brand and establishing lifelong impressions with everyone you meet at school. I would like to challenge you to become different by standing out from all the other students simply by being a *great student*. I would like to inspire you to take a leadership role in making your campus and community a better place to live.

Maybe by now you're getting the point of how important it is to show up ready for success in the classroom. Strive to brighten up every room you walk into!

You will become as small as your controlling desire or as great as your dominant aspiration.

~James Allen
Inspirational Author Best Known for *As A Man Thinketh*

An Excellent Example of Building Your Personal Brand

Here's a great example of how you should aspire to live your life on campus so that, when you graduate, your professors and your peers will say similar things about you. The following is taken from a **News Release from The University of Wisconsin-Eau Claire Campus** (with my emphasis by underlining):

Jasmine Wiley, University of Wisconsin-Eau Claire

Jasmine Wiley, Clintonville, a senior at the University of Wisconsin-Eau Claire, recently received the Scholar's Award from the University of Wisconsin School of Medicine and Public Health in Madison. The award amounts to $10,000 annually for four years.

"Since I grew up in rural Wisconsin, I know what it's like to live in a community that has a 'drive your tractor to school day,' where everyone knows your face if not your name," said Wiley. "I feel that I am well suited for rural medicine and would be happy to live in a small community and build my practice there. I have seen the need for physicians in these rural areas."

According to Dr. Julie Anderson, associate professor of biology at University of Wisconsin-Eau Claire, the scholarship award is based on achievement, life experiences, personal qualities, commitment and future potential as a physician, and nominations come from the medical school admissions committee.

"I first met Jasmine in the summer of 2006 as a orientation adviser when I typically meet over 100 incoming biology students," said Anderson. "Jasmine was a real stand-out that summer. She entered the University of Wisconsin-Eau Claire with an impressive high school record, but it was her maturity and excellent communication skills that gave me a lasting impression."

According to Anderson, Wiley also has demonstrated natural leadership abilities. She was president of the campus Pre-Med Club, for which Anderson is the faculty adviser. Anderson also worked closely with Wiley to organize and plan meetings, fundraisers and other activities. Wiley also has worked at the Chippewa Valley Free Clinic in Eau Claire and set up a link on the Pre-Med Club website so other interested pre-med students can more easily volunteer their services at the clinic.

"Establishing these connections and being involved in a variety of campus groups has helped make my experience at the University of Wisconsin-Eau Claire truly memorable and positive," said Wiley, who also served as a student academic apprentice in classes taught by Kelly Murray, lecturer in biology.

"During her time as a student I have seen Jasmine mature and become a real leader to her peers and a trusted collaborator to several faculty members in our department," said Murray. "Her academic record reflects her hard work and ability for success, and I have no doubt that this potential will translate well to medical school in her future."

Dr. Rick St. Germaine, professor of history, found Wiley to be "exceptionally motivated" to build a degree program rich in research and field experience. He supervised two of Wiley's independent study projects, one of which required her to do investigative field work on Menominee tribal resource sustainability. In another, she traveled to a Navajo Indian reservation in northern Arizona to provide medical policy and instructional assistance to a Navajo Indian school where St. Germaine serves as a staff-training specialist.

"Jasmine's drive, ambition, enthusiasm and exceptional teamwork resulted in an educational experience that will serve as a model for all future students," said St. Germaine. "We are going to miss her at University of Wisconsin-Eau Claire but take pride in knowing that her work in medicine will make a great contribution to the world."

"Brand Building" Key Words That Describe Jasmine Wiley

This write-up from the University of Wisconsin-Eau Claire Campus is a great example of the kinds of qualities that you should be striving to achieve in your own college experience. Here are the key words found in this press release that professors used to describe Jasmine Wiley:

- Achievement
- Life experiences
- Personal qualities
- Commitment
- Future potential
- A real stand-out
- Impressive high school record
- Her maturity
- Excellent communication skills
- Gave a lasting impression
- Involved in a variety of campus groups
- Memorable and positive
- Served as a student academic apprentice
- Become a real leader
- A trusted collaborator
- Her hard work
- Ability for success
- Exceptionally motivated
- Drive
- Ambition
- Exceptional teamwork
- A model for all future students
- Her work... will make a great contribution to the world

The preceding college story is a lot different than it would have been if Jasmine had made impressions similar to what some college students obsess about most of the time. *What if...*the following descriptions were used to describe Jasmine? Do you think the University would be writing about her with the same pride?

- Loves to party and can guzzle beer with the best
- Has all the latest iPods, stereo, and cell phones
- Dresses in the latest fashions
- Has a really neat car
- Most popular on campus
- Has the coolest boyfriend
- She's so weird she's cool
- Great tattoos and neat piercings
- Member of the THE sorority on campus

Compare the two lists of values and decide what values and character traits are really important to you!

Famous Dave's Key Lesson: Cultivate your Career's Reputation and your Personal Brand recognition now, while you are in college.

Become a Person of Values, Not a Person With Valuable Things
Your family and your friends are more important than having the latest fashion or car. Your values are more important than the latest trend. Your health is more important than popularity. Having respect and honor is always more important than wealth. If certain students find it's important to make their statement by having the latest car, the latest gadgets, the trendiest clothes, and flashing their money, just tell yourself that's great for them and be happy for them. But more importantly, be happy with yourself. Be grateful for whatever you have been blessed with.

You can find your happiness by being the best student you can be. If you approach every day with cheerfulness and you are nice and considerate to everyone you meet. If you are well-groomed, respectful of others, and show that you genuinely care about others, you will find your best friends this way—real friends, friends that you can depend upon and trust.

Jasmine Wiley's College Character Traits Will Follow Jasmine Throughout Her Career

The attitude, behavior, and work ethic that Jasmine demonstrates in college will set the course for the rest of her adult life. I can guarantee you that these character traits will be the same words that will be used in describing Jasmine throughout what will probably be a very stellar medical career.

Famous Dave's Key Lesson:
Creating the Value of Your Personal Brand

I sincerely believe the greatest value an employee brings to the marketplace is their ability to represent the company they work for, which in turn becomes their own brand-building value. Before a product becomes demanded in the marketplace, products are always first marketed by people. The person with the greatest personal recognition (their personal branding power) is chosen to represent the company and its product line. <u>Your highest value will always be determined by how influential you can be to the marketplace</u>. If you have little or no influence, you are a commodity whose only value is determined by how hard and how many hours you can work. In effect, simply, the more people you can make happy will determine the value and power of your personal brand.

Regardless of how you feel inside, always try to look like a winner. Even if you are behind, a sustained look of control and confidence can give you a mental edge that results in victory.

~Arthur Ashe
Legendary Tennis Player

ASK YOURSELF THIS KEY QUESTION ABOUT THE EFFECTIVENESS OF YOUR PERSONAL BRAND WITH COMPLETE AND BRUTAL HONESTY!

What would happen if you were to go into every one of your classrooms on the last day of college and ask your fellow students this question:

> *"Suppose you owned your own highly successful business and you desperately needed to hire someone. Would I be the first one you would hire?"*

The answer should guide your actions and behavior throughout your college years. Don't fool yourself here—it's important that you answer this question with brutal honesty! If you're not comfortable with the answer, or even with asking the question, this should help guide you on how to improve your personal brand recognition, classroom participation, and relationship skills while you are still in college. That's because, in college, you have four years to prove yourself, and if you can't get hired by your own classmates, what makes you think you will be on the short list to get hired in the real world? This is how important it is to cultivate your relationship skills and how you are going to show up every day in the classroom!

Famous Dave's Key Question: Look at yourself in a mirror and ask yourself: "What companies would want me representing them? Does my appearance represent the salary I should be earning? The only time this formula ever changes is when your intellectual creativity exceeds your appearance. So if you're not Albert Einstein, you'd better try to the best of your ability to look like Cindy Crawford or Brad Pitt!

COLLEGE SUCCESS TIPS: Your Personal Brand Called YOU, Inc.

1. Start building your personal brand in college. Your reputation, appearance, language, and behavior all contribute to the brand called YOU, Inc.
2. Your public relations skills that help get you recognized in the marketplace need to be practiced and lived out in college. Be very deliberate about how you establish your personal brand recognition.
3. Your value to the marketplace will be jumpstarted by the reputation you create while in college. Write down a list of character traits you need to start cultivating that will make you stand out from the masses.
4. Everyone you meet in college is important and they will be a key factor in how you are remembered. What kind of impressions are you creating?
5. Decide NOW how you want to be remembered. In college, you are developing the foundation for creating your life's personal brand.

SUCCESS SKILLS 101: How Will You Be Remembered? Write Out Your Own Press Release
Go online and get a template for a press release. Use Jasmine Wiley's newspaper press release to model your own. What kind of descriptive words would you like to be associated with when you graduate? How would you like your press release to read? After you have written out your press release, write down the values or character traits you used to describe yourself and by which you would like to best be remembered, and put these in your Vision Book. Reflect on them daily. Work towards living out these character traits as a driving motivator in your daily college life.

CHAPTER FIVE

Discover Your "Compelling Force" That Will Drive You Relentlessly Toward Success in College

Going from Report Cards to Paychecks is Tough Work... But So is Life!

College Is a Time to Aggressively Challenge Yourself Like You Have Never Done Before!

Jim Rohn, one of the world's great business philosophers, said, "Be easy on yourself and life will be tough on you. Be tough on yourself and life will be easy on you!" Jim also shared another profound thought: "Don't go where it is easy, you won't grow. Go where it is tough and you will grow into all that you can be!"

So...Why Are You Going to College?

Are you going because your parents said you have to go? Are you going to college so you can get a job? If you don't have a good reason why you are going to college, it is almost guaranteed that you will give up and drop out.

Identify One Compelling Force That Will Drive You Relentlessly to Succeed in College

To succeed in one of the most challenging endeavors of your life, it is best to have a compelling purpose that will drive you relentlessly until you have finished college. Ask yourself: "What is my compelling purpose that will force me to complete my college education? Why am I going to give up four years of my life and study harder than I have ever studied before?"

College Will Require Deep Sacrifices

What will compel you to give up fun things you could be doing to study every night and on weekends? Whether it is your dream to become a doctor, lawyer, teacher, politician, business owner, or community developer, make it a driving force in your life that will force you to stay in school and compel you to give every last ounce of energy to become the absolute best at your life's work.

List every compelling reason why you must stay in school and succeed. Here are some ideas; but make sure you find your own personal and meaningful compelling reasons:

1. I am going to college to fulfill my life's dream of becoming a _ _ _ _ _ _ _ _ _.
2. I am going to succeed in college because I am spending $40,000 and I don't like wasting my (or my parents') money! I know how hard they have worked (or I have worked) to send me to college and I am going to make sure I get the full value for my money.
3. I am going to college to better my chances in life. I don't want to live like my parents, living from paycheck to paycheck and just barely making ends meet.
4. I am going to college to wildly succeed so I can buy my parents a nice home for their retirement.
5. I am going to college because my parents have worked hard all their lives to give me this opportunity and I don't want to disappoint them.
6. I am going to college so that I can give my future family the best opportunities in life that I never had.
7. I am going to graduate successfully with the highest grades I can achieve, because I am a winner and I don't quit!
8. I am going to college to show the world how amazing and wonderful my ideas, skills, and talents are!
9. I am going to college because I want to use my skills, energy, and talents to make the world a better place

College Is Not Meant to Be Easy! It's Designed to Prepare You for Life—and Life Is Tough

Having a compelling purpose is critical, because college is designed to challenge you with learning situations that are seemingly impossible. Don't take this lightly! Half of all college freshmen will not graduate, and 24 percent will drop out in their first year. In addition, college life can be stressful, as you are being forced out of the security of your parents' home to live and interact with strangers. You will experience the loss of old friends and the challenge of making new friends. Make sure your major not only enhances your career but also is congruent with your life's passion. Your future is now your responsibility, and this should excite you!

Getting the Most Out of Your College Education Requires COMPLETE LIFE TRANSFORMATION

College is not about you being the same person just learning new things. College is about learning how to consistently and completely transform yourself into something greater. In the process, you will make good decisions and you will make some dumb decisions that will whack you. That's OK—sometimes it takes getting whacked for you to learn, and it's called education. If college doesn't dramatically transform your life into something greater and better, then you haven't put in the effort and you would be better off not wasting the money.

You must use your college experience to dramatically transform your life. Life is always going to be about change. Fear change and you will become its victim. Instead, embrace change, get out of your comfort zone, experience exciting new things, meet new people. Become the architect of an exciting, rewarding life of no limits!

The best years of your life are the ones in which you decide your problems are your own.
~Albert Ellis
Noted American Psychologist

Learn How to Take Care of Yourself

One of the toughest lessons you will learn about life is this: *LIFE is not happy camp and sitting around a campfire singing "Kum Ba Yah" with your best friends!* Life after college is filled with gut-wrenching problems and adversities. And you will also find out that there are a few people who just don't like you and actually find great enjoyment in your failures. Life is tough. Life is full of challenges and disappointments. Life is also full of some great times, some fun times, and some unbelievable opportunities. Whether your life after college is spent in frustration or accomplishment will depend on your attitude and your determination to succeed no matter what obstacles come your way. Decide you will live a great life!

You Don't Need to Be Einstein to Succeed in College!

It is common for everyone to question whether they have the smarts or the IQ to succeed in college. Much of your college success will come just from not procrastinating. Getting your work done before it's due is critical to your success. Start your assignments as soon as you can and finish as fast as you can. When you get your work done ahead of time, you have the luxury of checking it over, improving it, and getting everything right.

Get Ready to Fail and Embarrass Yourself!

I hope you fail and I hope you fail a lot! You must be thinking, *Am I hearing right?* Is this guy wishing me bad luck and failure? YES, YES, YES! I am wishing that you fail—but for your own wellbeing and success! If you are not pushing yourself outside of your comfort zone to risk failure, you'll never realize your greatest dreams. Your greatest learning lessons will come from failure, learning from your mistakes. If you are not making mistakes, you are not stretching yourself, and you will never find out what you are really capable of achieving.

> *If everything seems under control,*
> *you're not going fast enough!*
> ~Mario Andretti
> World's Greatest Race Car Driver

It's Really OK to Mess Up!

The best advice I can share with you is never to fear embarrassment. Many people never achieve greatness because they were afraid to try something for fear of what people might think of them if they messed up. It's out of failure and mistakes, however, that greatness is created! So go ahead and fail—try to see how far you can push yourself. And above all, don't be afraid of embarrassment.

> *I have discovered, the hard way, that success most often comes to the person who made the last mistake.*
> ~Famous Dave Anderson
> Founder of the World's Greatest BBQ Joint!

What You Think of Yourself Is Always More Important!

What really matters is not what others in your class think of you but what you think of yourself. You don't ever want to look back in life, living an unfulfilled life and regretting that you didn't try something when you had the opportunity.

Live the Life of Your Dreams!

Learn how to succeed now in college and you'll be able to live the life of your dreams. Experience the rewards and accomplishments of a job well done. Bring your ideas to life to make the world a better place. Become confident in your skills and ability to *stand up, stand out*, and *speak up* to separate yourself from all the other millions competing against you! You are unique. You are one of a kind. You are special. You are incredibly amazing!

> *Success doesn't just happen. It is forced into existence. To be successful, you must be determined to achieve your goal. You can't merely wish, hope, desire, or try real hard to succeed. You can't just have ambition. You must have a RAGE to succeed. You must have tunnel vision—a one-way ticket—do or die.*
> ~Larry A. Thompson
> Hollywood Film Producer and Talent Manager

Famous Dave's Key Lesson: Success and Caterpillars. The "struggle" is a critical part of your success journey. Don't expect to graduate and have the world handed to you on a silver platter. If your ambition is to be a top professional, you will have to work harder than everyone else. You will have to take more risks and do what others will not do. This struggle is what builds character and your fierce determination to not quit on yourself is what will help you achieve uncommon success. It's like an ugly caterpillar that eventually metamorphoses into a beautiful butterfly. We all start out as nothing, but slowly, over time, we transform into something incredibly brilliant and beautiful. But remember that the butterfly, when it is emerging from its cocoon, struggles and struggles nonstop until it is fully out of its protective casing. If you feel sorry for the butterfly while it is struggling, and you try to rescue it by pulling it out of its cocoon, you would kill it. The struggle itself is necessary to strengthen the butterfly's wings. Without the struggle, the butterfly dies. In life, we have to struggle to become all that we can become. Don't ever curse the struggle. Embrace it with optimism, knowing that the struggle is helping you become something incredibly brilliant and beautiful. After your struggles, you will be able to soar!

Life isn't about finding yourself.
Life is about creating yourself.
~George Bernard Shaw
Nobel Prize-Winning Author and Playwright

SUCCESS SKILLS 101: Your Dreams Are Spiritual Seeds of Greatness!
Never doubt yourself. There are many times when you naturally wonder if you will ever succeed. Don't let these doubts weigh on your confidence or belief in yourself. All successful people have doubts but work moment by moment to overcome these doubts. Your dreams are spiritual seeds of greatness that need to be nurtured and constantly fed a diet of optimism, love, generosity, and perseverance.

COLLEGE SUCCESS TIPS: Find one Compelling Purpose that will drive you relentlessly toward your success!

1. Identify one compelling reason that will drive you relentlessly to succeed in college. This reason must be so strong that you will never quit until you graduate.
2. Life is challenging. Learn to challenge yourself to greater heights of achievement. Always strive to take yourself to the next level.
3. Success in college, like in life, requires constant personal transformation. Strive to become a better you! Always be conscious of things you need to improve about yourself.
4. College, like life, is full of surprising twists and turns. Don't fear change. Embrace change and become the architect of your dreams.
5. Get your work done ASAP. Don't let procrastination be your downfall!
6. Don't fear failure or embarrassment. You will mess up and that's OK. True education is about making mistakes. The key is not to get down on yourself, but to pick yourself back up and get back into the game of life.

CHAPTER SIX

Don't Spend One Day
In College Without Goals

Definiteness of Purpose and the habit of Going the Extra Mile constitute a force which staggers the imagination of even the most imaginative of people.

~Napoleon Hill
Inspiring Author of *Think And Grow Rich*, in *The Master-Key to Riches*

Indecision Is Rocket Fuel for Procrastination.

Don't wait until you get hit with a lightning bolt of inspiration to complete your class assignments. Without daily "Must Get It Done" lists, weekly reminders, and a monthly calendar, you will wake up one morning realizing you've fallen way behind and there's no catching up. Notice I used "Must Get It Done" instead of "To Do"—just this change of emphasis makes all the difference!

College is all about personal responsibility to get your assignments done when they need to get done. Notice I said, *when they need to get done* and not *when they are due*! Cultivate the habit of getting your assignments done at least a day or two before they are due so you can go over your work several times before you turn in your assignment. Just this one strategy can mean the difference in a half grade or even a whole grade.

The change that is happening in the world today is so fast that the person who says it can't be done is blindsided by the person making a fortune doing it!

~Famous Dave Anderson
Founder of the World's Greatest BBQ Joint!

Success Is Simply Getting Things Done

If all you did was follow your plan for getting the things done when you said you were going to do them, you'd be ahead of the game. Success is doing the things you have to do when you need to get things done, consistently, day in and day out, no matter how much you may not like what you are doing.

What's Important NOW! The WIN Strategy

The drive to get things done is a critical character trait. Don't procrastinate. Don't get into the habit of putting things off until tomorrow. Do them now. Practice the **WIN** strategy: **W**hat's **I**mportant **N**ow. Whenever you are faced with multiple things to do, just ask yourself, "What's Important Now?"—and then get it done! Don't fall into the trap of always having to catch up. Remember: Get things done NOW!!!

Maximize Your Time

You are either productive or you are wasting time and money. Think consciously about how many hours you are wasting in a day. You must either be in class, studying, learning, creating, working, exercising, or having fun. Set some time aside to have fun and relax, but know the difference between relaxing activities and other mindless, unproductive activities like watching TV.

Make every second, every move, and every thought count. Time is your most valuable asset. You will never get a wasted moment back. Multi-task whenever you can. Always be thinking several steps ahead and organize your movements. Walk 25 percent faster, with purpose—make everyone keep up with you. *Be alert! Be observant! Know what's going on!*

> ***What you get by achieving your goals is not as important as what you become by achieving your goals.***
>
> ~Zig Ziglar
> International Leading Expert on Performance

Don't Do Nonproductive Things

Don't complicate your life with nonproductive things. Time is precious. Make every moment count. Many people live their lives in frustration because they major in minor things and don't focus on the major, important things in their lives.

Pat Riley, one of the NBA's greatest professional basketball coaches with 7 NBA World Championship titles, combed his hair slicked straight back, not out of fashion, but because he didn't want to waste valuable time combing his hair.

The WIN Strategy, and maximizing your time are great strategies that will give you the time you need to properly have fun and relax without the worry of whether you should be studying or completing a homework assignment. You will enjoy your college experience if you are not always playing catch-up and rushing to complete homework assignments. Time management disciplines will be critical assets to your career.

Start With Optimism!

Start out every semester with forward-looking optimism, believing that you are going to achieve the absolute best education. Believe you're going to get all your assignments done on time and even ahead of schedule! Believe you're going to achieve the best grades possible. Believe you're going to develop some really great relationships with classmates; and, just as importantly, believe you are going to have a great, fun time!

> *The greatest revolution of our generation is the discovery that human beings, by changing the inner attitudes of their minds, can change the outer aspects of their lives.*
> ~William James
> The Father of American Psychology

What Happened in the Past...Stays in the Past!

Don't fill your head with thoughts like how hard your courses are, or you didn't get the professor you wanted, or you miss home, etc., etc. Stuff like that will wear you out before you even get started!

Create the Future of Your Dreams!

Don't dwell on how hard things were back in high school. If you were never on the honor roll, if you were never an "A" student, that's all history. This is YOUR TIME NOW! Start believing that you are an "A" student. College is a fresh start. Reinvent yourself. Always be forward-looking. Don't fill your head with what happened in the past; stay focused on creating the future of your dreams! The most important mindset is absolute belief in your goals and unwavering hope for your future. Anything is possible!

Strive to Reach the Summit

Believe you have the ability to be an honor roll student. Envision your name on the Dean's List. See things positively and work towards your goals with positive optimism, unwavering confidence, and a sense of urgency. NEVER subscribe to the notion it's all right to be average. YOU ARE NOT AVERAGE! You are God's greatest miracle! You are amazing!

Besides, the definition of average means that you are either the *worst of the best* or the *best of the worst!* Always strive to be your best. Give your best effort in everything you do.

> ***Shoot for the moon. Even if you miss it you will land among the stars!***
>
> ~Les Brown
> World's Leading Expert on Personal Development

Setting Goals Requires You to Have a Plan for Your Life

Goals create definiteness of purpose and are critical to your success in life. If you don't have a plan for your life, how can you set meaningful goals? More importantly, if you don't have a plan for your life, you will fall prey to the plans of others. And guess what? The plans others have for you may not be good plans!

Goals Must Be Written Out

Setting goals is simple: Write down all the things you dream about. Here's the secret why some people live the lives of their dreams and others are still wishing: *You must write down your goals!*

<u>All goals must be written out and reviewed daily to keep you on track.</u> Keep them somewhere near your desk, where they can stay front and center. This is a great habit to get into, as your life will be lived according to goals. You will be hired to achieve your employer's goals. You will have goals for your personal life, and you will have goals for your family. Make sure you always write down your goals. Write down your top 6 goals on a 3-by-5 card that you carry with you at all times. Review them throughout the day.

> ***Control your destiny, or someone else will.***
> ~Jack Welch
> Legendary CEO of General Electric and Management Guru

URGENT: Before you do anything else, grab a pen and paper and start writing down your goals. ***Your goals should be meaningful enough that they stretch you and transform you.*** Don't spend another second of your life without written-down goals!

Survey Reveals Startling Truth! Writing Down Your Goals Will Give You A Head Start Over the Masses
Dr. Tony Alessandra, the world's leading expert on marketing and communications, cites a *Time* magazine survey that revealed that only 3 percent of the people surveyed had written out goals. And 97 percent had no goals at all or had only thought about them. They had not committed their goals to writing. So, if you want to stand out from the masses, all you have to do is spend serious time detailing in writing your goals. It has been said that most people spend more time planning their vacations than they do planning their lives!

Here's another interesting finding of this survey. The survey also estimated that the 3 percent who had written down their goals controlled 80 percent of the wealth.

Know How to Create SMART Goals

All goals that aren't specific or measurable are nothing more than hopeless wishes. Make all your goals SMART, an acronym for Specific, Measureable, Attainable, Realistic, Timely:

Specific. A goal that is clearly defined has a greater chance of being manifested into reality. A general goal may say, "I would like to lose weight." A specific goal answers six questions, such as: I will lose 10 pounds in two weeks by going to the gym every day for one hour so I can fit into my new tux and impress my girlfriend!

There are six questions to help you be Specific and define your goals:

1. **Who:** Who will be involved?
2. **What:** What do I want to do?
3. **Where:** Where will I do this?
4. **When:** When will this take place? *or* When it will it be finished?
5. **Which:** Which things are needed to make this happen?
6. **Why:** This is your compelling purpose

Measurable. Your goal must be measurable in terms of how much, how many, or specific outcomes. Lose 10 pounds in two weeks is a measurable goal. "Lose weight" is not measurable.

Attainable through Action. Your goal must be attainable through determined, massive action. You must start. Many people fail to achieve their goals because they never start.

Realistic. Your goal must be realistic and achievable within the time frame set. Can you lose almost one pound a day so that you will be able to lose the 10 pounds within two weeks?

Timely. You must place time frames on your goals, or else you will procrastinate and get into a habit of putting things off. Word to the wise: Even though you may have a set time frame, work to beat the time allowed. Get your stuff done early so you can review your work and make adjustments.

To help get you started, here are 30 great ideas for creating your own personal goals or ideals on your daily Must-Do lists:

1. Set a goal of a 3.75 grade average and work to beat this.
2. I am graduating with the absolute Best Grades Possible!
3. Make the honor roll and the Dean's List!
4. Start every day with optimism and cheerfulness.
5. Keep a vision book of my goals, my dreams.
6. Keep a journal and write down my best Million Dollar Ideas!
7. Manage my week using a Day-Timer and calendar
8. Use a daily Must-Do list rather than "things to do."
9. Keep my desk clean and all my papers filed.
10. Make every moment count and don't waste time.
11. Be on time for every class, arriving 10 minutes early to get the best seat and review class notes.
12. Get my homework done on time and work every day on my big term paper project.
13. Say "Hi!" to everyone and meet someone new every day.
14. Get a part-time job or internship to help reduce college debt while learning valuable job skills.
15. Identify and participate in extracurricular college activities and show enthusiastic team spirit.
16. Call home every Tuesday at 7:30 pm (or whatever day and time work best for you) and say hello to family.
17. Stay within my budget. I will spend no more than $_ _ _ every day, keep every receipt, and record all money spent.
18. Eat healthily and exercise to stay mentally and physically fit.
19. I will have fun!
20. I look forward to a very successful career that exceeds my wildest dreams!
21. I will use my talents and skills to make the world a better place!
22. I will live my life obsessively devoted to the service of others!
23. I will make my family proud of my accomplishments!
24. I will use all adversities as opportunities to demonstrate my unstoppable drive and determination to overcome all obstacles!
25. I will find the love of my dreams and experience an amazing life with this incredible person!
26. I will discover my greatest strength—my spirituality.

27. I will save everything I can to buy my first home. (Hint: Start a "my first home" fund your first day in college and religiously put something in it, even if it's only a dollar.)
28. I will learn how to speak in public.
29. I will learn how to sell, market, and promote.
30. I will be a leader in my community.

Every thought is a seed. If you plant crab apples, don't count on harvesting Golden Delicious.

~Bill Meyer
Radio Show Host

SUCCESS SKILLS 101: EXCEL AT SALES!
In thinking about your personal goals and what you want to accomplish in life, make learning how to sell one of your most important goals. I don't care what profession you choose—Marketing Yourself, Promoting Yourself, and Selling Yourself should be a mandatory course, no matter what your major may be! Your value to the marketplace is largely going to be dependent upon how well you are able to sell yourself, your ideas, your solutions, and your skills. You are always selling yourself! When you can sell yourself first, then you can sell anything. Unsuccessful salesmen think they are selling a product! The best thing you can do for your career is to take a debate class, join Toastmasters, and learn how to sell. *Being able to influence people with a call to action is a necessary skill in any field, profession, or leadership position.*

We are all salesmen, every day of our lives. We are selling our ideas, our plans, our energies, our enthusiasm, to those with whom we come in contact.

~Charles M. Schwab
19th- and 20th-Century American
Industrial Magnate, Founder of Bethlehem Steel

Create Your Own Personal VISION Book!

A Vision Book Gives Dimension and Reality to Your Goals and Dreams (just like scrapbooking on steroids!) Create a Vision Book for how you envision the incredible life of your dreams. Take a three-ring binder with pocket inserts. Place in this book your written goals and your list of 100 dreams. Make your vision real by cutting out pictures from magazines of your dream home, dream car, dream vacation, and really neat things you would like to do, such as hot-air ballooning, whitewater rafting, and so on. Next, paste these pictures into your Vision Book in a way that will inspire you. Have fun with it. Don't limit yourself. If you get any certificates of achievement, put them in a plastic sleeve or laminate them to preserve them; these go into your book, too. Cut out any articles that feature something you have accomplished and have been recognized for.

When you review your goals, also spend time reviewing your Vision Book to keep yourself inspired. Keep your dreams firmly planted in your mind. Keep your Vision Book updated with new goals. Anybody who has ever put together a Vision Book will tell you, this stuff works! I know practicing *visioning* and keeping a Vision Book has worked for me and it is surprising how your dreams become reality when your mind is focused with a clear vision on what you would like to have happen in your life.

> *Keep your dreams alive. Understand to achieve anything requires faith and belief in yourself, vision, hard work, determination, and dedication. Remember all things are possible for those who believe.*
>
> ~Gail Devers
> Three-time US Olympic Gold Medal Champion

FIVE MAJOR LIFE-PLANNING DOCUMENTS

There are five Major Life-Planning Manuals that you should have in your possession upon graduation.
These critical Life Planning Manuals create a framework for developing your life's design. Creating Life-Planning Manuals probably was not talked about in high school and probably will not be discussed in college. To my knowledge, I am the only employer and life coach advocating that all college graduates should start creating these Life-Planning Manuals while in college. Thank your lucky stars you have this book, because these Life Manuals will be invaluable for creating the life of your dreams.

Collecting the information that fills these Life Manuals will be YOUR responsibility. You should not leave college without a Life Plan for your life, goals you want to accomplish, and a budget to support yourself. It's amazing that we let college graduates out into the world without a plan for their lives, much less not even an inkling about how to create a budget to manage their finances!

The following is an outline of the five Major Life-Planning Manuals, detailing what should go into each Life Manual.
Collect this information with the help of your parents, who may have vital information you will need, and keep it in a three-ring binder. This Life Plan Manual, along with your Vision Book, goals, and your journals should be kept under lock and key. These manuals are living, breathing documents. They need to be updated regularly and kept within easy reach, where you can review them to see how you are progressing. They are not supposed to be completed, tucked away, and then forgotten about. They will be your foundation for creating an exciting and rewarding life of unlimited opportunity!

LIFE MANUAL #1: YOUR LIFE PLAN—A Life Map of "How You Are Going to Manifest Your Dreams Into Reality!"

- **A Written List of 100 Dreams** (everything is possible!)
- **Your Goals Written Down**
  Detailed, written-down, measurable goals with time frames
  -Spiritual Goals
  -Family Goals
  -Career Goals
  -Financial Goals
  -Health and Fitness Goals
  -Social Goals

- **A Vision Book**
  -Your dream home
  -Your dream car
  -Your dream job
  -Your dream vacation
  -Adventurous things you would like to try
  -Anything else related to envisioning your dreams

- **A List of Your Professional Resources**
  -Insurance—Life and Disability
  -CPA/Accountant
  -Financial Planner and Advisor
  -Banker
  -Public Relations
  -Professional Photographer
  -Wordsmith (to help write or edit critical documents: resume, reports, etc.)
  -Computer and Technology Expert
  -Website and Internet Support

- **List of Accomplishments**
- **Community Involvement and Charity**
- **Political Awareness and Involvement**

LIFE MANUAL #2: HEALTH CARE *(Your car has a service and repair log. Don't you think you should, too?)*
- Detailed Record/Portfolio of Personal Health Records
- List of Professional Healthcare Resources
  -Family Doctor
  -Dentist
  -Specialist
  -Nutritionist
- Once-a-Year Complete Physical
- Health and Dental Insurance
- Nutritional Plan
- Physical Fitness Plan

LIFE MANUAL #3: CAREER PLAN
- Finding the One Thing You Love to Do In Life—start collecting pertinent information regarding your future career
- Updated Resume
- Keeping an Updated Address Book and Email List—Become A Powerhouse Networker
- List of Mentors and Role Models
- Professional Associations
- Continuing Career Education
  -Evening Courses
  -Industry Conferences
  -List of Industry Periodicals and Magazines
  -Seminars, Lectures, and Trainings
- Career Benchmarks and Related Accomplishments

LIFE MANUAL #4: FINANCIAL PLAN
- Buying My First Home. (How much, what does it look like?)
- Development of Investment Portfolio
  -Long-Term Investments (that you never touch!)
  -Short-Term Investments (for large-ticket items like your first car)
  -Emergency Money Fund
- Detailed Yearly Budget Corresponding to Life Plan
- Charitable Giving
- Will and Estate Planning

LIFE MANUAL #5: MENTAL AND SPIRITUAL DEVELOPMENT GROWTH PLAN

- Continuing Education in All Areas of Personal Interest
  - -Music
  - -Cooking
  - -Dancing
  - -Language
  - -Art
- Spiritual Growth
  - -Discover your greatest resource—your spirituality
  - -Personal mentorship relationship with spiritual leader
  - -Be an integral part of a worshipping community
  - -Share your spiritual journey with youth

If a man is called to be a street sweeper, he should sweep streets even as Michelangelo painted, Beethoven composed music, or Shakespeare wrote poetry. He should sweep streets so well that all the hosts of heaven and earth will pause to say, "Here lived a great street sweeper, who did his job well."

~Dr. Martin Luther King Jr.

SUCCESS SKILLS 101: Take Massive Action!

All successful people will tell you to write down your goals. Very successful people visualize their goals throughout the day. Highly successful people develop the discipline to carry out their goals. *Here's the key lesson*: They all work their butts off!

A plan is no good if it sits on a shelf collecting dust. Every day, you must be conscious about keeping yourself motivated. You cannot achieve any of your goals without taking **MASSIVE ACTION**. Visualization is required to keep you focused on your goals. Action manifests your goals into reality. You must be willing to work harder than anyone else . You must be willing to be the pacesetter and make others keep up with you. Nothing will ever happen until you take action and make it happen. Don't ever hesitate. Push yourself beyond expectation. Deliver more than what was expected. Don't ever wait for someone to tell you to get going! Take pride in being a self-starter!

COLLEGE SUCCESS TIPS: Set yourself apart from the masses by having dreams, a vision, and written-down goals!

1. Don't spend one day in college without goals. Your future success depends on you getting full use out of your college investment. Goals will give meaning to your college courses.
2. Indecision is rocket fuel for procrastination. Have daily Must-Do Lists, Weekly Reminders, and a Monthly Calendar. Being organized is a great life skill!
3. Getting things done when they need to get done will jumpstart your success. Develop a reputation for being someone people can count on for getting things done.
4. Don't waste your time doing things that are not important to your success. Always ask yourself, "**W**hat's **I**mportant **N**ow?" Practicing the WIN strategy will keep your life focused.
5. Create a list of dreams and a vision for your life. Turn your dreams into goals by writing them down using the SMART method of creating goals. Goals not written down are nothing more than wishes!
6. What happens in the past, stays in the past. Stay focused on a positive, richly rewarding future.
7. Create a Vision Book for manifesting into reality the life of your dreams! Cut out pictures of your dream job, your dream home, your dream car, your dream vacations, and other neat stuff that will make your life incredible!
8. Start developing your Five Major Life-Planning Manuals. You will want to graduate having these five manuals started and filled out as much as possible. These five manuals will be the foundation for creating the life of your dreams!

There is an epitaph in Boot Hill Cemetery in Tombstone, Arizona, which reads, "Here likes Jack Williams; he done his damnedest. What more can a person do?

~Harry Truman
33rd President of the United States

CHAPTER SEVEN

Visualize Your Goals

Visualizing Your Success Strengthens Your Confidence
The secret to goal-setting that produces over-the-top results is to see yourself successfully living out your goals *as if they were already achieved*. You must never doubt your ability to achieve your goals. Every cell of your body must be fully immersed in your vision. Peak performers learn how to visualize their success in every move they make. Successful athletes spend significant amounts of time visualizing their routines and winning. Entrepreneurs visualize building new businesses and creating new products and services. Community and world leaders visualize what is possible for their people. Get a good head start in life by mastering *how to visualize your success!*

Visualize Your College Success
Visualize yourself in class asking questions and participating with positive energy. Don't ever let self-doubt hold you back from participating. Keep a firm picture in your mind of yourself successfully graduating and seeing how proud your family will be of your achievement! Keep this vision firmly in your mind. Then, throughout the day make sure you reinforce your visualization by spending a few minutes in mental concentration. The positive vision you hold of yourself is stronger than any outside negative influences. Keep focused on the positive!

If you can dream it, you can do it!
~Walt Disney
Filmmaker and founder of The Walt Disney Company

A Focused, Goal-Driven Mind Is Stronger Than Any Other Force Known to Man

World-class achievers—who are unstoppable and seemingly possess superhuman energy to manifest their dreams into reality while overcoming all impossible adversities—are driven by a force stronger than anything known to man: a focused, goal-driven mind. All doubt is banished from their minds. The thought of quitting never enters their minds. They expect no other outcome but success. Setbacks are never taken seriously but only considered as stepping-stones to success.

World-class achievers envision their success; they can taste it, hear it, feel it, and experience it as if it already has been achieved. Their minds, bodies, spirits, and every cell of their beings has but only one purpose: to work in harmony to fulfill their visions. A focused, goal-driven mind is the only thing that separates the achievers from the non-achievers. Achievers possess optimistic, solution-conscious minds that focus on abundance and what can be; and non-achievers possess negative, problem-conscious minds that focus on scarcity and all that has gone wrong. Achievers are forward-looking. Non-achievers are always looking backwards.

Your Mind Is the Most Precious, Valuable Asset You Possess!

Protect your mind. Never let negative people influence your thinking. Never let adversities fill your mind. Keep your mind focused on your future. Keep your mind focused on your goals. Never let your mind's incredible energy be used for worry, self-doubt, or self-pity. Turbo-charge your future by using your mind's amazing energy to focus exclusively on your dreams, vision, and goals.

> *The greater danger for most of us is not that our aim is too high and we miss it, but that it is too low and we hit it.*
> ~Michelangelo
> Legendary Italian Renaissance Painter, Sculptor, and Architect

DON'T GIVE SUBSTANCE TO YOUR PROBLEMS!
In Other Words, Don't Visualize Your Worries Into Reality!

IMPORTANT: *Believe that yesterday's problems are in the past and tomorrow is a fresh start.* Start your day out right. When you get up in the morning, immediately spend the first few minutes visualizing your day. See yourself greeting everyone you meet with a big, cheerful smile. Visualize having a great day! There will be times when it seems like the whole world has collapsed on you. Don't spend your positive creative energy feeling sorry for yourself when you need to be focusing all your energy setting yourself up for a comeback! Protect the vision you have of your future. Your positive energy is much more productive when used to create a better future—not reliving past mistakes or failures. Your ability to visualize a positive solution and see yourself overcoming your setbacks will be vital to creating new hope for a better future.

Don't Cloud Your Incredible Tomorrows With Yesterday's Crap!

When you go to bed, don't dwell on bad things that already happened. As hard as it is, you have to remove all destructive thoughts from your mind forever!

Have you ever noticed how some people just seem to have a dark cloud hanging over them, and no matter how hard they try they always seem to have all the bad luck? It's because they have allowed negative thinking to overwhelm their minds. Reliving bad things can have the same effect of attracting more bad things into your life. Focus on a better tomorrow and remember: *Things will always get better with a positive optimistic outlook!* So, before you nod off, be grateful; say thanks to your Creator for all your blessings. Go to sleep with a smile on your face! Do this every day and, at the end of a year, you will be amazed at how many of your goals will have been successfully manifested into reality.

COLLEGE SUCCESS TIPS: Visualization helps program your mind to a successful course of action!

1. Visualizing your success is a key step in turning your goals into reality. Visualize every important thing, every step that needs to be done, and envision how everything successfully comes together. Think through everything beforehand, programming your mind to access your subconscious "zone power." Your zone power gets activated when your vision is so powerful it focuses every cell of your body, your strength, your wisdom, and your soul into working in harmony, manifesting your vision into reality.

2. The key to visualization is to see yourself successfully completing the task as if it has already happened. Successful athletes visualize hitting the mark and winning the game. Visualize your success. Visualize your achievements.

3. Don't give substance to your problems by visualizing your worries! Be careful to focus only on your success.

4. The vision you hold firmly in your mind will drive you relentlessly towards your goal. Once you have your vision, then act upon it with confidence!

> *I noticed an almost universal trait among Super Achievers, and it was what I call Sensory Goal Vision. These people knew what they wanted out of life, and they could sense it multi-dimensionally before they ever had it. They could not only see it, but also taste it, smell it, and imagine the sounds and emotions associated with it. They pre-lived it before they had it. And the sharp, sensory vision became a powerful driving force in their lives.*
>
> ~Steve Devore
> Personal-Achievement Expert

CHAPTER EIGHT

Follow Your Dreams and Pursue Your Passion

You have to find something that you love enough to be able to take risks, jump over the hurdles, and break through the brick walls that are always going to be placed in front of you. If you don't have that kind of feeling for what it is you're doing, you'll stop at the first giant hurdle.

~George Lucas
American Filmmaker Best Known for *Star Wars*

The Best Advice Ever for Creating the Life of Your Dreams
Find your passion in life. Don't waste your college investment doing something you don't absolutely love doing. Life is too short. Don't spend a lifetime fulfilling someone else's dreams. If you absolutely love what you are doing, you'll never work another day in your life again! When you love what you do for a living, you will jump out of bed every morning looking forward to work! Work is no longer work. Your work becomes the love of your life—it's your life's passion.

If You Don't Know What Thrills You, Give Everything You Do An All-Out Effort. Only Then Will the Universe Reveal What You Were Meant to Do in Life!
Some students are blessed by knowing what thrills them and they know exactly what they want to do in life. If this is not you, however, here's my best advice: Even if you don't know what you want to do in your adult life, that doesn't mean that you should approach college with a "let's just check it out" attitude. You need to take the basic required courses and pour 100 percent of an all-out effort into doing your absolute best, and here's why...

The Universe Honors Those Who Strive to Give Their Best

Usually, when you are unleashing an all-out effort, your calling in life will come find you. It seems like the universe waits to see if you are worthy of your calling. It also seems that if you approach life with casualness, not knowing what you want to do, no real direction in life, then there's a good chance your life will end up in confusion. Casualness always leads to mediocrity. When you give everything your best *all-out effort*, however, your life's calling will eventually be made known to you.

> *In the homes of poor people you'll find a big TV. In the homes of wealthy people you'll find a big library.*
>
> ~ Jim Rohn
> America's Foremost Business Philosopher

Don't Take A Hobby and Turn It Into Your Profession—Unless You Can Totally Master It and BECOME One of the World's Best

Be brutally honest about the difference between "what you are good at" and "what you like to do." You may like to listen to music, but that doesn't mean you should make a career out of it. Whatever you choose, you need to be very passionate about it, so much so that you are willing to discipline yourself to become a professional and master your craft. Be realistic about what you like to do. If you hated math in high school and you struggled with it... don't fool yourself into choosing a profession that requires you to be a whiz at math in college. You should love what you do so much that you are willing to eat, drink, and sleep your profession 24 hours a day.

Startling Harvard Research About Your True Passion in Life!

In 1960, Mark Albion, a Harvard professor, studied 1,500 students from the Harvard Business School. Upon graduation, 83 percent of the graduates, or 1,245 in Group A, pursued careers that had the biggest opportunity for wealth and status, regardless of whether or not that was their life's passion. The other 17 percent, or 255 in Group B, decided to follow their dreams and pursue their true passions in life, whether or not their work brought riches or fame.

Twenty years later, in 1980, Professor Mark Albion resurveyed the 1,500 graduates. The results were astonishing! There were 201 millionaires, but only one of them was from Group A! That means that out of the original 255 in Group B, almost the entire group became millionaires through following their passions! Clear, convincing evidence of why it is so important to follow your dreams and pursue your true passion in life. I am not suggesting you pursue your passion for the sole purposes of becoming a millionaire, but here's the thing: When you are devoted to your craft and you become excellent at making many people happy with your products or services, they will reward you exceedingly well—beyond your wildest dreams!

Creating the Life of Your Dreams!
Creating your life's plan is like building a building. You need a vision of what the building is going to look like. A building needs a master plan and your life needs a master plan. And much like your life, how grand your building will soar will depend upon how deep the foundation is that supports the size of the building. Think of the building that is above ground as your vision; it's how you present yourself to the community and it's how the community perceives you to be. The building's foundation is what people don't see, but it's critical to the size of the structure above ground. Your foundation, what people can't see, are your values, internal strength, the character traits that make you unique, and your drive—everything that gives rise to your success and supports your vision.

Go confidently in the direction of your dreams! Live the life you've imagined.

~Henry David Thoreau
Noted American Author and Philosopher

DID YOU KNOW EVERY INDUSTRY HAS MANY DIFFERENT CAREER OPPORTUNITIES?

Most college students have no idea how vast and varied the different type of career opportunities are available in any particular field. When they declare their majors, most students have an idea that maybe they would like to be in advertising, for example; but they may not be aware of all the different kinds of jobs there are in advertising. If a particular field interests you, make it your point to research all the available career opportunities or job titles that are related to this industry or profession.

Examples of Career Opportunities Within the Advertising Industry

Knowing all the career opportunities that are available may help you discover if your interests, talents, or skills are better suited to a certain job skill within this field. For example, advertising offers jobs in the following areas:

- Creative (developing great ad ideas)
- Copy Writing
- Art Direction
- Illustration
- Commercial Photography
- Production
- Media Buying
- Campaign Manager
- Advertising Sales or Account Executive
- Public Relations
- Social Media Strategy

If your job is boring, it's because you are boring. Find a job you love and there won't be enough hours in the week!

~James W. Anderson
Entrepreneur, Speaker, and Author

Examples of Career Opportunities Within the Restaurant Industry

Since I am in the restaurant industry, I know there are a ton of different opportunities available to someone interested in the restaurant and hospitality field. Here are a few examples:

- Restaurant Management
- Chef
- Wait Staff
- Hosts
- Kitchen Management
- Customer Service
- Catering Manager
- Food and Beverage Manager
- Bar Manager
- Accounting and Bookkeeping
- Franchise Management
- Diet and Nutrition
- Menu Recipe Development
- Food Science
- Creative Menu Design
- Restaurant Design
- Kitchen Design
- Food Safety
- Restaurant Equipment Sales
- Wholesale Food Sales
- Food Distribution

The number of job titles in the restaurant industry alone can be overwhelming. That is why it is so important to pursue a number of internships for you to get a good inside look at jobs that are better suited to your talents or skills.

I find television very educating. Every time somebody turns on the set, I go into the other room and read a book!

~Groucho Marx
Early Film and Television Comedy Star

SUCCESS SKILLS 101: Don't Be Afraid to Pay Your Dues!
If your employer recommends you start at the bottom, DO IT! Just because you're going to be a college graduate doesn't give you the right to bypass the "you've got to pay your dues" jobs where you will gain "this is how you succeed in this business" knowledge. If this means starting at the bottom, *start at the bottom!* Just because you will have a degree doesn't mean you have the chops to move immediately into management. Many careers have been ruined because young recruits got themselves into positions in which they were destined to fail because they weren't "seasoned" in all the nuances of the job. Gaining on-the-job experience is another reason why you want to intern: You want to give yourself a good head start by the time you graduate.

Here Are 18 Questions to Help You Discover What's Important to You or Your Passion In Life

First, with brutal honesty to yourself, answer these questions, remembering Shakespeare's wisdom: "To thine own self be true" ! don't put down answers that your parents would approve of. Write down the answers that are only important to you. It's absolutely important that you take the time to write out your answers. Just looking at the questions is not enough. As you write out the answers, you will start to see a pattern that could be useful to your career choice. Answering these questions will help you decide your career path and the college courses you will need.

1. If money were no object and failure could never happen, what would you do in life? What do you envision your life to be like in two years, five years, ten years?

2. Is there one thing in your life that, if you could change it or remove it, would dramatically change your life for the better?

3. Are there any fears that hold you back that make you want to try to smash through your self-limiting thoughts?

4. What interests you? What do you spend most of your time thinking about? (And guys, don't say girls!)

5. What are the interests of the friends that you like hanging around with? Do you like to do the same things?

6. Do you have any talents that you enjoy?

7. How do you spend your free time?

8. Do you like being around other people and do you have an easy time talking with people you may not know?

9. What were your most favorite classes in high school?

10. What were the classes you hated the most?

11. Do you think that you are more creative or more analytical? Were you good in math and science, or did you favor art and drama, or sports?

12. Do you have any favorite hobbies and, if so, what interests you about them?

13. Are there certain activities that frustrate you?

14. What are your favorite types of books to read? Do you love reading and researching topics that catch your interest?

15. Are there any sports that fascinate you? Are you athletic? Do you prefer working with your hands?

16. Are there certain types of TV shows that interest you, and why?

17. Are there any national public figures that interest you and you would like to meet or learn more about? Does the profession of these people interest you?

18. What would you like people to know about you?

**For more information on how to choose a career you'll love, check out this great website...
www.rockportinstitute.com**

Here's Where Everything Starts Coming Together

Take the answers to these 18 questions to your career advisor. Your findings, along with the advice from your career advisor, will not only give you a great head start in helping you choose several career choices but also help you narrow down your major or the courses you need to be taking. I am not saying this is always possible, but it might be just that slight edge of difference that gives you your direction in life and makes all the difference in your college success.

Famous Dave's Key Lesson: Believe you are on a mission from God. Think about your career not as a job but as a calling.

> *We're on a mission from God!*
> ~Jake and Elwood
> The Blues Brothers

Start Cultivating the Thinking, Behaviors, and Attitude of Your Future Profession

Once you have a good idea what profession you would like to pursue, start thinking and behaving like you were already successful as one of the top leaders in your profession. You probably also know someone who is very successful in this profession. How do they think and behave?

If you want to be a lawyer, start thinking and behaving like a very successful lawyer. Join an attorney's trade association. Ask a successful attorney out for lunch and have him or her tell you what you should be learning in college. The same holds true if you want to be a doctor, professor, politician, entrepreneur, or whatever profession sets you on fire. Study how the successful go about crafting their careers and begin this journey in college.

> *People think I'm disciplined. It is not discipline. It is devotion. There is a great difference.*
> ~Luciano Pavarotti
> World's Greatest Italian Tenor

What If You Don't Have a Profession Picked Out?
Make SUCCESS Your Major!

Don't despair if you haven't figured out your major; just visualize yourself being a "highly successful person." Make "success" your major. Just think about how all successful people think and act. What are the work habits of a successful person? Even though you may not have a career picked out, you can still develop the thinking and behavior of successful people. This will give you a jumpstart once you do find your passion in life.

Turbo-Charge Your Career By Learning These Highly Valuable Career Skills Even If You Don't Know What You Would Like to Do for the Rest of Your Life!

Get a running head start in your career with these critical job skills that are transferable to any profession or industry. When you become a master of them, you will have job skills that will be highly invaluable to you throughout your fabulous career!

- If you are independent and a self-starter: Take *Entrepreneurship*-related courses. In today's business environment, many companies are outsourcing jobs that used to be done internally. And there are many small companies that specialize in meeting these needs, but they need technical and creative help. Many of your best job opportunities are not with large companies but small companies with steady growth, filling specialized niches.

- If you are outward-going and enjoy meeting people: Take *Marketing and Public Relations* courses. Learning how to sell ideas and market and promote your company and its products will be a very financially rewarding skill anywhere you go. Executives who have mastered the art of selling are the highest paid in the world!

- If you love math and enjoy numbers: Take *Basic Accounting and Math*. You may not want to be an accountant, but knowing how to read financial statements will always be a highly sought after skill in all professions.

- If, throughout your high school years, you have noticed that people naturally gravitate towards you and you have held leadership positions in high school: Take *Leadership* and *Management* courses. The leadership, management, and team-building skills you will learn will help put you on the fast track once you decide on your profession.

- For any profession, *communication skills* are a must: Take effective *Writing, Journalism, Sales, Public Speaking*, and *Debate* courses. There are many other similar courses, all of which will serve you immeasurably in any line of work. You'll look back with gratitude and thank your lucky stars you took communications courses in college!

- Similarly, for any profession or industry, *technology skills* are highly desired. Make sure your college is technologically up-to-date and relevant. You will be immediately put on the short list if you have technology-relevant training. *Data Management, Social Media, Digital Communications, Website Management*: All these courses are necessary in today's digital marketplace. Take as many technology courses as your brain allows!

- You'll hear me saying over and over again: *Learn how to create value.* It's fundamental to anyone's success. Even if you haven't found your life's calling, work hard to create more value than what you are paid. Everything you touch, make it better. Don't spend one day living in the negative. If you produce more than you consume, you will always be in demand. This is the secret to having employers lined up at your doorstep!

Far better it is to dare mighty things, to win glorious triumphs, even though checkered by failure, than to take rank with those poor spirits who neither enjoy much nor suffer much, because they live in the gray twilight that knows neither victory nor defeat.

~Theodore Roosevelt
26th President of the United States

COLLEGE SUCCESS TIPS: Determining your profession for life will give meaning to your college courses.

1. Don't spend a lifetime doing something that you don't love to do! Follow your passion and become the world's best at doing what you love to do.
2. If you don't know what you want to do in life, give everything you do 100 percent of your effort. When you give everything total, full-out effort, the universe will know you are ready and it will then reveal your true calling in life.
3. Once you have determined your future passion, make it a point to find out all the various jobs that are available within that industry. A certain job within that field may be more suited to your interests.
4. Jumpstart your career by acting and behaving like a very successful professional in that industry. Get involved in the industry. Go to industry conventions and trade shows. Subscribe to the industry publications.
5. If you still don't know your life's profession, then just start acting and behaving like a very successful professional. It's important that you cultivate successful career and living habits even while in college.
6. Don't be afraid to start at the bottom and work your way up. Learn everything you can about your profession. Pay your dues! The experience will be invaluable when you are in a leadership position.

> *When I started my own first business at age 19, many people thought I was still in school and would often ask me what I was studying. I replied, "I am studying Success 101: Achievement, Success, and Accomplishment. I am working on my MBA—a Massive Bank Account!"*
>
> ~Famous Dave Anderson
> Founder of the World's Greatest BBQ Joint

CHAPTER NINE

The 19 Most Critical Character Traits Employers Look for in Graduates

Talent is cheaper than table salt. What separates the successful individual from the talented one is a lot of hard work.

~Stephan King
American Best-Selling Author

What Employers Look for In a College Graduate

Getting a job today is more competitive than ever before! In my 35 years of being in business, I have hired many key employees and have looked through thousands of resumes. Today, college graduates are competing for jobs not just against other graduates from American colleges and universities, but now they are competing against bright, eager, hardworking graduates from around the world.

When I am asked, "What do you think about when hiring someone?" I have found that just knowing how to do a job is not enough. A business will absolutely fail if the business does not have passionate, enthusiastic, driven people who believe they are winners working to create a profitable and successful business. The attitude of the whole team is what drives the business towards success and profitability. Character, passion, energy, teamwork, and know-how—all are critical ingredients to look for in a new hire.

The Successful Employer Hires Not for the Job But for the Successful Long-Term Well-Being of the Whole Company

As an employer, I would never hire someone just for "the job." I hire someone for the successful well-being of the whole company. You think to yourself, Will this college graduate help our company achieve greater success and greater profitability? Will this college graduate be the best, raving loyal ambassador for our company? Will this graduate contribute to our team?

It Is the Graduate's Responsibility to Understand Why These Character Traits Are Critical to a Company's Success

Over the years, I have found that the best hires almost always share the same character traits. And, hopefully, my sharing these character traits will jumpstart students into a better understanding of what they should be learning while in college and what will be expected of them once they are on the job.

After 35 years in business, I have found that what's critical to hiring a new employee hasn't changed no matter how fast the world's marketplace is changing. A person's character should always be steadfast and unwavering! I share these thoughts as an entrepreneur, employer, and someone who has created over 20,000 new jobs and hired many key employees in his career...

Here Are the 19 Most Critical Character Traits Employers In a College Graduate:

1. **THE RIGHT ATTITUDE**

   My number one goal: We Hire Smiles! I want to hire cheerful young people with high energy, enthusiasm, and a positive attitude. These people brighten a room when they walk in and they are a joy to be around. They enjoy life and do not fall apart when confronted by challenges. They are no-limit people. Everything is possible! The person with the right attitude is optimistic about finding solutions and not defeated by problems. You can be talented, smart, and a hard worker; but if your attitude stinks and you are negative, you can do more harm to an organization or business.

I will take someone with the right attitude any day over someone with smarts and a negative attitude! Positive, enthusiastic people are great contributors to the organization's team spirit!

2. **SHOW UP READY FOR SUCCESS**
   One of the major differences between the successful and the unsuccessful is that the successful have a clear understanding of how they are supposed to show up ready for success (work). Successful employees dress sharp and are immaculately groomed. Their attitudes are cheerful and optimistic. Their language is positive, upbeat, and optimistic. The energy of successful-minded employees is contagious, and they empower everyone around them! Employers delightfully parade these employees in front of investors, clients, and other potential new hires. College graduates are expected to *stand out* from the masses of everyday workers.

3. **PASSIONATELY DEVOTED TO WHAT THEY LOVE TO DO FOR THEIR CAREER**
   I want to hire energetic people who are passionate about what they love to do in life. They embrace their work with a fierce passion to be the best so they can provide the best service or the best product to others. They love what they do because they understand how this one thing they love to do makes someone happy and the world a better place.

4. **SELF-STARTERS**
   I want to hire motivated self-starters, people who don't need to be told what to do and who naturally always look for things to do in order to stay busy. Self-starters hate just sitting around doing nothing. These people are also the first ones to jump up and volunteer when needed. They show up early and work until the job is done. They always keep busy. They are pacesetters and expect all others to keep up with them. They challenge themselves to keep getting better and they put into practice the number-one secret to all success in life: *Give more than is expected*!

5. **WILLINGNESS TO LEARN**

    I want to hire open-minded people who are trainable, coachable, and possess an eager willingness to learn. They are willing to learn my company's way of doing business and willing to embrace our precepts for doing business. You will never hear "I know that" coming out of these naturally curious people! I appreciate people who have a lifelong commitment to self-learning and transformation.

6. **GREAT PEOPLE SKILLS**

    The question is: *Can I build a team around this person or will this person be a great contributor to the team?* I look for people with great relationship skills who are a breath of fresh air to be around. These people are cheerful, positive team members who eagerly contribute and support their team. Above all, they absolutely do not engage in gossip! They realize that gossip is the quickest way to break apart a team. Instead, they are good-finders—always looking for the good in others. But most importantly, I want to know if this person has the ability to navigate in social settings with our clients, vendors, suppliers, investors, and potential new customers.

7. **PERSONALLY COMMITTED TO RESEARCH AND DEVELOPMENT IN THEIR CAREER AND PERSONAL LIFE**

    I like to find self-motivated people who have strong personal commitments to their own growth and personal development. They don't wait for the company to train them—they eagerly read monthly trade journals, they take night courses, they attend seminars, lectures, and other industry-related trainings. They have a drive to stay on top of their profession including being technologically up-to-date.

8. **GREAT NOTE-TAKING SKILLS**

    I get concerned about hiring people who don't take notes. I love people who take great notes. Developing great note-taking skills begins in college. When a professor is standing in front of a class, it is very noticeable who takes notes and who doesn't! I can absolutely guarantee you every employer, when hosting a meeting, will immediately notice who takes notes and who doesn't!

I have never seen a great manager or leader who does not take notes! No one can remember all the details of important meetings without great note-taking. I also believe it is a lack of respect to all the other team members if someone is not taking notes in a meeting. You cannot successfully grow an organization without having things written down to share with your team. A word to the wise: I have personally been saved, and have seen many other executives I know saved, by having a paper trail of great notes when confronted by a critical issue. TAKE NOTES!!!

9. GREAT ANALYTICAL SKILLS

Is this person able to figure out the problem? Do they have good research and problem-solving skills? Are they able to gather support to solve a problem? Are they problem-conscious or solution-conscious? Can they develop and implement a solution? Is this person detail-oriented and are they organized? Great analytical skills come from doing your homework and being thoroughly knowledgeable about your craft.

10. GREAT CREATIVE SKILLS

Is this person creative? Do they see things that others do not see? I love to hire no-limit people who think outside the box and find new and exciting ways to build business or create new products. Creative people are always seeking new ways to create better ways to serve the customer or to make the business more productive and profitable.

You are not born creative! Creativity comes from being passionate about your profession and exposing yourself to knowing everything about your industry. The more you know, the more creative you can be!

> *Education is not rote repetition. Education in its truest form inspires courage to try something new. Education removes fear. Creativity is what happens when fear is not allowed to occupy valuable mind space!*
>
> ~Famous Dave Anderson
> Founder of the World's Greatest BBQ Joint!

11. GREAT PERSUASIVE PRESENTATION SKILLS

Can this person write and can they effectively communicate in front of groups? I need to know if this person will be an effective, raving, loyal ambassador for my company. Will this person be an effective communicator to our investors, stakeholders, customers, clients, other team members, and the public? I want to hire enthusiastic people who have great confidence in their presentation skills. Can they inspire and influence others to a call to action?

12. EMBRACES HEALTHY HABITS WITH NO ADDICTIONS

While I understand this is not a question I can ask as an employer, it is my desire to hire healthy, energetic people without addictions. I want to hire non-smoking people who are well-adjusted at home, without any alcohol or drug dependencies.

I appreciate people who love to exercise. These people are more positive, eager to participate in things, and more fun to be around. Smokers are always noticeable when they have to disappear to grab a quick smoke! People who have destructive habits and who do not exercise drive up the costs of health insurance for all employees and rob the business coffers of valuable financial assets, which could have been used to grow the company.

Healthy employees are more mentally alert and are more productive. Healthy employees have strong, passionate enthusiasm, ambition, and nonstop drive.

13. SKILLFUL IN MANAGING THEIR FINANCIAL AFFAIRS

Here's another question you can't ask about; but, in a perfect world, I want to hire people who are personally financially responsible.

It's difficult to hire people who have financial problems at home, because their money woes carry into the workplace. Employees who can't handle their personal finances at home usually are the whiners, gossipers, and complainers; and, they generally believe the company is responsible for their money woes. Employees who carefully manage their personal financial affairs will also be good caretakers of the company's assets.

14. COMMITTED TO CREATING PROFIT

Strange as it may seem, many employees are personally afraid of thinking they are responsible for "creating profit!" I like to find people who clearly embrace the fact that they are engaged in the business of creating profit and they know how their work creates profit for the company. Profit is simply leaving something better than when you found it—adding value. Profit is created when you give more than what is expected of you and are paid to do.

15. STRONG WORK ETHICS

I want to hire self-motivated people who have strong work ethics, people who understand their success depends on contributing more than they were hired to do. They get to work early and are the last ones to leave. They are not clock-watchers. They are the first to volunteer. They always give more than 100 percent of their effort. They take great pride in their work. They take great pride in serving others. **Famous Dave's "Inside Secret" to Success:** *Average employees work just to get a paycheck. Great employees understand that the fundamental basis of "work" is to create value for others.*

16. PERSONAL VALUES, ETHICS, AND STANDARDS

Today more than ever, I look for people of great character, people who have high standards. We need individuals who work to cultivate personal values, principals, and moral standards. Trust, integrity, honesty, and loyalty are valuable commodities in today's workforce. When they tell you something, you believe them and you trust them.

17. STRONG COMMUNITY SPIRIT

I like to hire community-minded people who are active in their communities. I feel it's important to find caring people who understand the importance of getting involved. I appreciate people who genuinely care and are not apathetic to the requirements of developing strong communities. Community-minded people help nurture the youth in their communities. They vote and they are committed to doing whatever it takes to build strong local government. Strong communities are needed for businesses to thrive.

18. GENEROUS GIVERS

A critical lesson in life is to come to a complete understanding that *it isn't about you!* Success is all about bettering the lives of others. Obsessive, devoted service to other people. Giving more than is expected. Delighting beyond expectation. Sharing knowledge. Always helping those around them succeed. People who generously give of their time, finances, expertise, ideas, and resources have discovered the greatest secret to success: It's all about giving to make the world a better place.

> *What is the use of living, if it be not to strive for noble causes and to make this muddled world a better place for those who will live in it after we are gone?*
> ~Sir Winston Churchill
> Legendary Prime Minister of Great Britain

19. TECHNOLOGY COMPETENCY AND RELEVANCE

Here's a new one: the 19th critical character trait or skill today's employers look for Technology Competency. You must be relevant to what's happening in technology. Today, you have to have information technology skills, social media skills, and knowledge of how to market through the digital universe. Today's marketplace has a voracious appetite for graduates who are capable of navigating the digital global highways of unlimited information. Don't show up on a job interview with old-fashioned technology, as you will scream to the world that you are already outdated and prehistoric! (Your outdated cell phone could trip you up!)

Use your college years, as your opportunity to develop the most important character traits that will define your success in life. Your grades, relationships with your professors and faculty, and participation in various college activities (basically, your Personal Brand's reputation) must reflect these character traits. Your future employers will be looking for evidence of these character traits on your resume, in your interviews, and from the people who recommend you.

COLLEGE SUCCESS TIPS: Start now to cultivate the most important 19 critical character traits employers look for in a college graduate!

1. A positive, optimistic, cheerful attitude.
2. Show up ready for success (work).
3. You love what you do for a living.
4. You must be a self-starter.
5. You must be willing to learn, be teachable, and coachable.
6. You must have great people skills.
7. You must be committed to personal research and development in your career and in your personal life.
8. You must have great note-taking skills.
9. You must have great analytical skills to figure things out.
10. You must have creative skills to innovate, change, and improve.
11. You must have great persuasive presentation skills.
12. You must embrace healthy habits, with no addictions.
13. Financial Responsibility: You must be skillful in managing your own personal financial affairs.
14. You must be committed to creating profits.
15. You must possess a strong work ethic, willing to do whatever it takes.
16. You must have strong personal values, ethics, and high standards.
17. You must have a strong community spirit.
18. You must have a generous heart.
19. You must be technology-relevant and competent.

> *Formal education will make you a living;*
> *self-education will make you a fortune.*
> ~Jim Rohn
> America's Foremost Business Philosopher

CHAPTER TEN

Before You Begin College... Write Out Your Resume and Job Recommendations

Start College By Writing Out Your Resume!
Most students starting out in college have never seen a proper resume! By the time you graduate, you better be prepared to create the best resume ever written, one that will get you noticed and hired. I highly suggest you study how to write a great resume, because quite frankly it's your resume that will get you hired, not your diploma! This is not a book on how to write resumes; there are plenty of great websites that can help you. However, I wholeheartedly recommend writing out your resume before you start college. Just the process of writing out a great resume will quickly demonstrate how important it is to gain a powerhouse of experiences in college besides just getting good grades.

Keep Your Resume Updated and Ready to Go at All Times
I will urge you to keep a professional-looking resume ready at all times. You can use your resume to show to your advisors or to a professor how important it is for you to get into a class that may be hard to get into. In addition, while in college, you will meet many influential people. Get used to sending an *It was nice to meet you* note. You never know when this may turn into an opportunity for an internship or a job opportunity. Developing a job-ready resume is just as important as getting your report card—if not more important, because it's your resume that will get you an interview and, hopefully, hired!

Write Out a "You're Crazy If You Don't Hire This Amazing College Graduate" Job Recommendation

In addition to learning how to create a great resume, it is also critical that you start learning what it takes to be worthy of a *great job recommendation*. Think about when you are ready to graduate and you are asking a professor for a job recommendation. What would you like your professors to say about you?

> *Great job recommendations just don't happen, they need to be cultivated throughout your years in college!*
>
> ~James W. Anderson
> Entrepreneur, Speaker, and Author

Once you have written out your job recommendation, spend the next four years of college fulfilling all the great stuff you put down on your recommendation. Writing out what you think your ultimate job recommendation would look like is a good exercise in determining what experiences and activities you need to participate in while attending college. What goes on your resume and job recommendation will also help you decide how important it is for you to fulfill a leadership role in the school organizations you might want to join.

> *The closest to perfection a person ever comes is when he fills out a job application form.*
>
> ~Stanley J. Randall
> Outstanding Canadian Businessman and Political Leader

Here is a Great Sample Job Recommendation...

To Whom It May Concern:

Hi! This is Professor Smarterthanawhip, I have been asked to give a letter of recommendation for a remarkable graduate, Mr. Joe Graduate (your name), and I am highly honored to provide my recommendation. Joe has not only been one of our outstanding students, but he has also helped contribute his own over-the-top, inspiring spark of team spirit and leadership to our campus.

Mr. Joe Graduate was a standout student who brought passion, a great work ethic, and dedication to every aspect of his college experience. A hard-working, honor roll student, Joe has demonstrated great communication skills with his professors, faculty, and fellow students. Joe was the President of the Debate Team, leading his team to the Intercollegiate Finals and winning top honors. I have been equally impressed by Joe's dedication to physical fitness, as he participated in several cross-country relay marathons.

I personally took interest in Joe when he was experiencing a tough time with challenges at home and balancing his desire to do well at school. To Joe's credit, Joe recognized he needed help and didn't hesitate to go to his advisors. Many students tend to try and handle these situations on their own, and that is why the dropout rate in college is so high. I watched as Joe worked through each issue with growing maturity, which gives me the confidence to be recommending Joe to your business. I admire students who are able to work through their challenges with optimism and determination. As Joe continues to grow, these character traits will serve Joe well in many leadership positions.

Joe is selfless, and a great team player, always helping and inspiring those around him. It is for these reasons that I am highly recommending Mr. Joe Graduate. I believe sincerely that Mr. Joe Graduate will be a terrific asset to any team, business, or organization. I guarantee someday you'll be able to look back with pride and say, "We were the lucky company to have given that young man his first start in life!" Please feel free to contact me for further references.

Sincerely,
Professor Smarterthanawhip
Collegeville, USA

Use Life's Challenges to Your Best Advantage

Notice how I also included a tough challenge in the job recommendation for Mr. Joe Graduate. You never want to have your recommendations or resumes just filled with nothing but rosy accolades. Employers want to know how you are able handle life's challenges. The best employees are not just hard workers or smart; the real value in great employees is how they handle problems. How they deal with the stress that comes from intense adversities that all businesses experience at some time during the course of the marketplace's ups and downs is of real interest to an employer. And a real "great find" is an employee who can inspire fellow co-workers through the challenges and help the business retain its productivity, profitability, and clients through the thick and thin. This is why it is so important that you don't give up or drop out as a result of tough times during your college years.

If you think about your college experience as prep work for developing a great job recommendation, the reality of landing the job of your dreams will be surprisingly easy!

~Famous Dave Anderson
Founder of the World's Greatest BBQ Joint

Famous Dave's Key Lesson: Writing out your resume and job recommendation when you first get to college will help you think through the courses, projects, activities, and internships you need to participate in during your college years. This will help you develop the best resume and the BEST job recommendations possible!

For true success ask yourself these four questions: Why? Why not? Why not me? Why not now?

~James Allen
Inspirational Author Best Known for *As A Man Thinketh*

SUCCESS SKILLS 101: Start A Photo Success Library
Here's a great idea for you to start developing while in college: A Photo Success Library of all your achievements, awards, travels, interesting people including celebrities you meet, community involvement and career-building activities. Only pictures of you with interesting people should be posed pictures. The other pictures you want to be activity shots of you actively involved in helping to make the world a better place. These pictures should have compelling captions or taglines that trumpet your character traits; but do it in a way that makes you look humanitarian, not arrogant. The best pictures should be of you working with your team on some challenging task. Your pictures, arranged in a professional photo album, may be something you might want to consider leaving with a prospective employer or recruiter. DON'T leave something that is nothing but a bunch of pictures of you with all your awards, as this is self-serving and indulgent. If used properly, your pictures could be a big help in getting you hired!

God gives every bird its food,
but He does not throw it into the nest!
~Josiah Gilbert Holland
19th-century American Novelist and Poet

CHAPTER ELEVEN

Your First Day of College is Actually Your First Day on the Job!

The #1 Secret to Making the Most Out of Your College Years, Jumpstarting Your Career, and Living a Life of Unlimited Opportunity...Is to Treat College as if It Were Your Job!

Turn Your Report Card Into Your Paycheck

I sincerely believe the number-one secret to setting the foundation for an amazing life filled with adventure, unlimited opportunities, and the career of your dreams is to begin, right from day one, treating college like it was your first job. Start thinking about your report card as your paycheck!

Treat College as if It Were the Best Job You've Ever Had!

Quit thinking academia, college, and school. And start thinking career, boss, and potential client. Start thinking about everyone you meet in school as if they might be your boss, co-workers, or potential clients. This will affect how you prepare yourself, how you dress, how you behave, and how you treat others in college. Think that every professor might be your future boss and they might be able to hire you right after graduation. Think every classmate is a potential client or someone who you might want on your resume for personal recommendations. These thoughts alone should cause you to pay attention to the people you meet. Thinking "job opportunity" rather than "college" is one change in thought that will jumpstart your career right from day one when you start school!

Proof Why You Must Impress Everyone You Meet In College:

*27% of all "successful hires"
are done through referral.*
~careerXroads.com

So the question is: *How are you impressing people in school, and will they hire you or will they recommend you?*

Your College Experience Should Be Resume-Building

Think about your college experience as resume-building. Striving just to get straight A's will not put you on top of the short list for getting hired. Employers will look at how well you "played nice in the sandbox." They will check out your team spirit, how well you participated in college activities, and the diversity of your experiences in college. From your first day in college, you need to be strategizing about what extracurricular college activities would look best on your resume for your intended profession.

Famous Dave's Key Lesson: Job skills are practiced and mastered while in college. Don't kid yourself that after you graduate, you'll get serious and really buckle down. If you don't have the discipline in college now, you'll never get it in the real world— and that's a fact, Jack!

Treat Every Day As If It Were Your First Day On the Job

If you just landed the job of your dreams and you knew this job could lead to unlimited income and opportunity, *how would you show up*? Would you be concerned about making sure everyone was excited that you were hired? Would you have your best smile on? Would you be overly respectful and courteous to everyone you meet? Would you be striving to make the best impressions and to have everyone think highly of you? Behaving as if each day is your first day on the job is how *every day* at college should be for you. Surprise your employer and be fully prepared to make your first day count when you get hired. Don't be like all the other new recruits who behave like they are fish out of water.

It's OK to Be Yourself!

Let's first begin by understanding that you are YOU! Many students have a tough time in school because they compare themselves to other students and even try their hardest to be like them. All students want to be liked, accepted, and they don't want to appear to be dumb or not cool. You're in school to get good grades, yes; but your social skills, "playing nice in the sand box," is also important. Here's the most important lesson: Always be you! *Don't squash your own potential by trying to be someone else.*

Your Future Employers Will Be Wondering What Makes You So Special and Why They Should Hire You

If you are envious of other kids in your class and you try to be like them, you're not concentrating on the wonderful giftedness you were blessed with. God made you wonderfully different. Explore what makes you unique. Discover your untapped talents and skills. Your employers are looking for "your personal slight edge" that gives you the difference over all the other job applicants. If you look and behave exactly like everyone else, how are you going to stand out from all the other millions of kids competing for your job? You don't have to be radically different, but you need to be just you. Most often, just giving everything you do a little extra effort will put you head and shoulders over everyone else!

You were born an original.
Don't live like a copy!
~Jonathan Sprinkles
Inspiring Speaker and Author

COLLEGE SUCCESS TIPS: Here Are 10 Ways Your College Experience Will Be Considered for Employment

1. Your attendance will be a direct reflection of how you will show up for your real-world job.
2. Your hard work, effort, and willingness to sacrifice to do your best in college will be a huge indicator to a future employer of your work ethic and self-discipline.
3. How you prepare and show up for your classes will be a good indicator of your ambition to be fully prepared for your real-world job.
4. Your attitude and behavior in college will be very telling of how you will respect your real-world job and other employees.
5. Your team spirit, passion, and enthusiasm at college will be very telling of what kind of team player you will be at work. Your enthusiasm will indicate what type of raving, loyal ambassador you will be for the company that hires you. GO TEAM!!!
6. Your involvement in college activities will be a good indication of how supportive you will be of your company's employee programs. *Get involved, don't sit on the sidelines, make things happen!*
7. Your willingness to speak up in class and share your viewpoints, or your willingness to ask questions in the classroom, will provide your employer good insight into your ability to promote the company to customers, suppliers, and stakeholders.
8. How you handle setbacks, both academically and personally, will be very telling of how well you can handle stress, challenges, and setbacks in your real-world job.
9. How you respect and follow directions from your professors will be very telling of how you will respect and follow directions from your boss.
10. Treat your report card like it was your paycheck. Your grades are not up to your professor, they are up to you. The same holds true in real life: What's on your paycheck is not up to your boss, it's up to you and how good you are at your job!

CHAPTER TWELVE

Famous Dave's "Inside Secret" to Success...
My Personal $10,000,000 Powerhouse Introduction!

I started out with nothing and it has been my passion and enthusiasm that has opened more doors and gotten me more than $10,000,000 of free publicity in my business career. I have been featured on Oprah Winfrey, Regis and Kathy Lee, CNBC's The Big Idea, The Food Network, The Discovery Channel, The Travel Channel, ABC, CBS, NBC, PBS, and over 300 radio channels! Be proud of you who are. You are amazing! You are special! Your ideas could change the world! Tell the world who you are!!!!!! Look what it's done for me!!!!!!!!!!!!!!!!

Learn How to Introduce Yourself and Others Properly
Have you seen parents ask their kid to tell someone their name, and the kid is so shy they squirm, don't look the person in the eyes, refuse to share their name, and then turn and try to hide behind their parents? Unfortunately, this is how many college students introduce themselves! Learn how to introduce yourself properly and let the world know that you have arrived!

Generally, when students are asked to share their names, they really don't know how to reply. For example...

"What's your name?" Answer... "Mary."
"How are you?" Answer... "Oh, pretty good, I guess."

Your Introduction Should Be Impressive and Memorable

Personally, when I introduce myself, I say with passion and enthusiasm: *"Hi! I'm Famous Dave, Founder of Famous Dave's of America, Legendary Real Pit Barbeque, the World's Best Barbeque Joint and America's Best Tasting Ribs. My whole purpose in life is just to make you happy! You can check me out on FamousDaveAnderson.com, Facebook, or LinkedIn."*

When asked how I am doing, I reply:

"I am better than ever! I am rockin' and a rollin', hunky dory, feeling groovy, settin' the world on fire, got a tiger by the tail, if I felt any better they would have to call the pOOleece!" (No that's not a typo, that's how I say it—wouldn't sound good if I just said "police!")

My Powerhouse Introduction may seem over-the-top. And yes, it is! In today's highly competitive environment, you have to stand out from the "Sea of Sameness!" I have gotten into more doors and have been able to get more than $10 million dollars worth of free publicity because I have learned how to set the world on fire just with how I introduce myself!

Famous Dave's Key Lesson: Get into the habit of being memorable when introducing yourself, and finishing off by remembering to share your personal website, Facebook, Twitter, or LinkedIn addresses.

It usually takes me more than three weeks to prepare a good impromptu speech.

~Mark Twain
Legendary American Author and Humorist

Learn Famous Dave's 30 Second Power Introduction and Learn How to Famously Shake Hands

Most people call this a "30 second elevator speech." I don't like to call it an elevator speech because it reminds me of boring, sleepy, elevator music—that's why I call it a "30 Second Power Introduction!" This will require you to get out of your comfort zone. I want to brighten up the room when I introduce myself. Learning how to give a Famous Handshake that is warm and inviting will do more to create long-lasting relationships that will help jumpstart your career.

- Tell the folks who you are, while reaching out to give a warm, inviting, firm handshake. Firm doesn't mean vise grip—make sure you get this right. You don't want to shake hands like a dead fish, either!
- Tell folks a little something about yourself.
- Tell where you are going to school and something about your school.
- Share your major and your career plans.
- Finish your personal power introduction by sharing your personal website and other social media connections.
- Give your newfound friends your business card.

When introducing yourself, always speak up so everyone can hear. Share your introduction with some cheerfulness and say it with a big smile! It should go something like this:

Tell who you are:
Hi, my name is Famous Dave Anderson.

Tell folks something about yourself:
I was born and raised in Chicago and I am a big Cubs fan.

Tell where you are going to school and something about your school:
I am going to the University of Wisconsin, Madison Campus, home of Bucky the Badger.

Share your major and your career plans:
I am taking Success 101: Achievement and Accomplishment, and my second major is Journalism. And I have a secret ambition, and it's to write for The New York Times!

End your introduction by giving your personal website:
You can check me out at www.famousdaveanderson.com, and I am also on Facebook, Twitter, and LinkedIn

If you don't know your major or your career plans, tell folks that you are studying success. This will make them stand up and take notice of you, because I can almost guarantee that they have never heard this before from a college student!
I am majoring in Success 101: Achievement and Accomplishment and I am exploring several other majors. I like business but I also like journalism, but most importantly I am working my butt off to make every second count!

My advice here is that you just don't say you are "undecided" or you haven't made up your mind. This signals to someone that you might be unable to make decisions.

From now on, always, always, always—with no exceptions—give your 30 Second Power Introduction, even when you are among friends, in class, meeting professors, or with anyone outside of your fellow students. This needs to be your introduction, absolutely no exceptions! Don't give in to shortening this up around friends. Your friends may laugh, but explain you are using them to practice!

GREAT CAREER ADVICE: Go Overboard When Introducing Your Friends

When you have the opportunity to introduce your friends, you should share as much information about them as you can. Your ability to get to know your friends and promote them this way will yield dividends, especially once you are in a work-related situation. When you introduce your friends always share as much knowledge as possible about them; be effusive, complimentary, and build them up. This will do wonders for your friendships. You are practicing a vital life skill that will do wonders for your career.

Here's an example:

This is my good friend, Joe College. He is a second-year student here at the University of Wisconsin, studying Success just like I am. Joe is one of the university's finest students and has big plans to make the world a better place. Just my friendship alone with Joe has made my coming to the University of Wisconsin the best decision I've ever made!

Everyone has an invisible sign hanging from their neck saying, "Make me feel important." Never forget this message when working with people.

~Mary Kay Ash
Founder, Mary Kay Cosmetics

COLLEGE SUCCESS TIPS: Let the world know that you have arrived!

1. Learn how to introduce yourself properly and leave everyone impressed that they had the opportunity to meet you!
2. Learn Famous Dave's $10,000,000 Powerhouse Introduction and use it with gusto! *Don't chicken out!!!*
3. Always tell folks something about yourself in your introduction. Finish by telling them how they can contact you through social media.
4. Learn how to introduce your friends and make them look like they are VIPs and celebrities! This skill alone will do wonders for your career.
5. If you don't yet know what you are going to do after college, don't let this keep you from delivering an over-the-top Powerhouse Introduction. Just tell them that you are studying Success 101!

If you have a good name, if you are right more often than you are wrong, if your children respect you, if your grandchildren are glad to see you, if your friends can count on you and you can count on them in time of trouble, if you can face your God and say "I have done my best," then you are a success.

~Ann Landers
America's Advice Columnist

CHAPTER THIRTEEN

The "Leading Edge Difference" That Will Have Your Professors Talking You Up All Over Campus!

Just this one strategy will guarantee you an unfair advantage over all other students competing for the best job recommendations and will help you land your dream job!

It is often said that America is "The Land of Opportunity." But opportunity must be carved out of the impossible by common folk who are willing to work long hard impossible hours. Believers, who find strength when there is none left. Going the extra mile after all others have quit. This is the slight edge of difference that separates mediocrity from excellence, winners from losers, and the wealthy from the poor.

You don't conquer the mountain all at once. You don't eat an elephant in one bite. The secret to success is making small consistent improvements daily. Improving something every day, no matter how small, creates forward momentum that builds and builds and builds until your effort yields huge results! Many thought-leaders often call going the extra mile the "Slight Edge Difference" because all it takes is just a little bit more effort every day to set yourself apart from the masses. I prefer calling this extra effort the *"Leading Edge Difference"* because it's what will help you stand out from the masses, giving you the Leading Edge over your competition, and will help set you up for unlimited success throughout your life!

The Leading Edge Strategy: Show Up Ready for Success.
This one strategy can improve your grades one grade point average higher WITHOUT any more hard work or studying! It's all about your *presence in the classroom*. Show up every day like it was your first day on the job and this will be the Leading Edge difference between an "A" and a "B" Grade!

How You SHOW UP Means More Than You Think!
Since I am constantly being asked to come and share my entrepreneurial success story with high school students and college students, I have come to understand what all teachers and professors know about their class and what you absolutely should know about *YOUR PRESENCE* in the classroom!

All teachers know immediately who the best students are and which students are just going to squeak by—without ever really knowing them! They instinctively know this by your presence, involvement, and behavior in the classroom.

When I am teaching and standing in front of a room full of students, it is so easy to see who is engaged and wanting to learn—including the fact that it's also very easy to see the students who wished they were somewhere else!

The difference between great people and everyone else is that great people create their lives actively, while everyone else is created by their lives, passively waiting to see where life takes them next.
~Michael E. Gerber
Bestselling author on Entrepreneurship

Consider These Two Scenarios...

SCENARIO 1: The Typical *"I'm Here for the Good Times"* College Student Imagine if you were a professor, and you had a student who had a tendency of just making it to class and had a habit of sitting in the back rows of your class. Then, the student sits all slouched over the chair and dressed like they just rolled out of bed.

They look bored and without a doubt such a student wishes they were someplace else. This student keeps nodding off, has a tough time keeping their eyes open, and occasionally lets out a big, wide, gaping yawn without bothering to cover their mouth. They avoid your stares and are constantly engaged in giggling gossip with surrounding classmates. They rarely take notes. They never ask questions or raise their hands to answer a question. When class is over, they rush out as if the classroom was on fire!

SCENARIO 2: The *"I'll Do Whatever It Takes"* College Student
Now, you have another student who, before the semester gets going, makes an appointment with you to go over the syllabus and make sure they understand what is expected from them—and they also share why they are taking your course. This student then shares that they are looking forward to learning a lot from you—and now, as their professor, you feel like you are invested in their success. This student takes great pride in their appearance and gets to class early. Right from the start, you feel this student is destined to become a leader. They sit up with good posture in their chair. They are alert, attentive, and follow everything you say. They ask relevant questions and are quick to engage in classroom discussions. And you can't help but notice this student is always scribbling away furiously taking notes. As a professor, you love to see students actively taking lots of notes.

Famous Dave's Key Lesson: With all things being equal and both of these students fairly bright just to have gotten into college in the first place, which one do you think will always get the benefit of the doubt—when there is a slight difference whether a student gets an A or a B on homework or on a test, and the decision is up to the Professor? Who do you think will always get the better grade? The answer is obvious: the student who shows up, is well prepared, ready for success in the classroom. Who do you think will get the best job recommendations? Who do you think will get top consideration for a hard-to-get-into class?

Which student are you?

> **SUCCESS SKILLS 101: Learn the Proper Skills Required to Take Care of Your Appearance**
> Learn how to stand and sit with the proper posture. Learn how to properly wash, fold, or iron your clothes. Learn how to dress for success. Shine your shoes. Learn proper manners and etiquette. Above all, be respectful and address your elders appropriately. There's good stuff on YouTube. Find demonstrations of these skills and practice them. *Your appearance is just as important as your diploma and needs to be studied with the same intensity as you would study for the best grades possible!*

Prepare yourself for success...

If you're not practicing, somebody else is, somewhere, and he'll be ready to take your job.

~ Brooks Robinson
Baseball Hall-of-Famer

Just How Important Is the Way You Show UP?

In a July 19, 2010 article in <u>USA Today</u>, reporter Brian Mansfield covered the beginning of auditions in Nashville for the forthcoming season of "American Idol," for which 16,000 people had already gathered by 4 a.m. Thursday morning for auditions that were formally set to start on Saturday. But, as Mansfield reported, those waiting were already being auditioned without their knowing it, since supervising producer Patrick Lynn was strolling through the crowd with a small video camera, looking for people who caught his attention among the mostly sleeping crowd. "We tell people all the time," Mansfield reported Lynn saying, "If they're standing out, even almost by not thinking about it, then they're going to do well inside. So if somebody has brought five or six of their friends, and they're playing guitar, especially if they're talking to each other and one person is always the center of attention, I like to gravitate toward those people."

You Never Know Who Is Checking You Out!

This newspaper feature article about "American Idol" auditions and how people are judging you to see if you stand out is proof that you are always being scrutinized, whether you want it or not. College is no different. Your professors, other classmates, job recruiters visiting campus, are always on the lookout for students who stand out. How are you showing up every day for college?

> *People say you should never judge a book by its cover. This is true...but you also want to make sure someone is compelled to pick up the book!*
>
> ~James W. Anderson
> Entrepreneur, Speaker, and Author

College Is Where You Start Learning How to Set Yourself Apart From The Masses

Don't sabotage your success in college by your casualness, just because you can. Don't ever behave and dress like the other students just to fit in. Remember, your whole goal is to set yourself apart—to stand up and stand out from the masses to create unlimited opportunities for yourself. Treat your classroom with casualness and you might be one of life's unfortunate casualties. Give yourself every fighting chance you can to guarantee your success in school and that will give you the jumpstart you will need in your career!

College IS "The Real World!"

Make up your mind right from the get-go that you are going to show up *like you will be expected to show up for work*—well-rested, neatly dressed, ready, and properly prepared for work. You are ready for success. Remember, the "real world" doesn't start after college. "College IS the real world!"

Even I don't wake up looking like Cindy Crawford!
~Cindy Crawford
One of the world's most beautiful women

SUCCESS SKILLS 101: Go the Extra Mile!

The Leading Edge Difference is often going the extra mile to do things that others are unwilling to do. Pay a little extra attention to your appearance and go to class prepared to learn. Just because your professors aren't going to police you like your parents, doesn't mean you can take college casually. I am sure your parents would have stopped you before you left the house and said, "Get back up to your room and clean yourself up! You're not going to school looking like that!!!" Starting in college, it is now your responsibility to show up ready for success.

THIS IS IMPORTANT: There Is No Job Security In Life. No One Is Owed a Career and No One Is Owed a Job!

You don't go to college so you can get a good-paying job when you graduate. That is the wrong thinking! You go to college to learn the skills required to be a professional or a master at your craft. Excellence, being *the best of the best*, and learning *how to be increasingly productive and profitable* is what gives you value in the marketplace, *not* the degree. Your degree just gives you a foot in the door. What you have learned in college is almost obsolete by the time you graduate. It's always going to be your drive and your ability to create your best Slight Edge Difference over everyone else that creates your value in the marketplace.

Just remember: With all this talk about competitiveness, your best opportunity for success still comes from helping others achieve a better life. Creating the Slight Edge sets yourself apart from the masses, who are aggressively trying to drown you out so they get noticed first. Competition makes you more creative, makes you work harder, and brings out your best!

> *Job security is gone. The driving force of a career must come from the individual.*
>
> ~Dr. Homa Bahrami
> International Business Lecturer

How You Show Up Begins With Your ATTITUDE!

Whether you show up casually or you show up determined to make the most out of college is determined by one thing only: your ATTITUDE! Your attitude is determined by the choices you make every morning when you get up. If you have a great attitude, you will be determined to have a great day. If you have a lousy attitude, you will show up with casualness and a "whatever" attitude. Walk 25 percent faster, and it will make you look like a person on a mission. Spend a little extra time on your homework. Be the first to volunteer. Do extra-credit homework. Some of the greatest races were won by hundredths of a second! All it took to win and get placed in the record books for history was just a little bit more effort. Go the extra mile!

The Dynamics of Sitting In the Front Rows!

HERE'S WHY IT'S SO IMPORTANT TO BE A FRONT ROW SEATER

In my business career, I have come to believe that "Front Row Seaters" are only 20 percent of the total work force, yet these people are responsible for 80 percent of the productivity in any business. I have also noticed that when I am participating in business meetings, conferences, and seminars, that a good majority of attendees still carry over bad habits from their school days, as they scurry to sit in the back-row seats like a bunch of immature kids. While at a glance this may seem totally inconsequential to your career's success, I disagree wholeheartedly! I feel so strongly about this that today I only want to hire "Front Row Seaters," and here's why: Front Row Seaters signal to the world that they are showing up, standing up, and *ready to take on the world*!

Front Row Seaters Strive to Be First in Life

Front Row Seaters believe they deserve to sit in the front rows of life. They have a VIP mindset, believing they belong in the best seats in the house—the front rows are where they belong, front and center. Front Row Seaters have positive attitudes and love associating with other positive "can do" people in the front rows. Sitting in general admission, lost in the back rows, or stuck in the "nosebleed balcony seats" is unthinkable to a Front Row Seater!

Front Row Seaters Show Up Ready

You can also be pretty sure the people who sit in the front rows are healthier, because their Front Row Seating mindset also requires them to be in top physical condition to support their peak performance drive. Front Row Seaters take great pride in their almost perfect high attendance rate as they hate for their teachers to notice if, *God forbid*, they happen to miss a class! This is a great character trait that translates to an employee that you can depend upon and trust. You know they are going to show up and be prepared for a productive day's work. Front Row Seaters will control the financial markets of the world!

Front Row Seaters Are Leaders

The students who sit in the front rows will be tomorrow's leaders driving the marketplace; they are leaders in their communities, and they are the ones who step up to make the world a better place. Front Row Seaters are eager, they are ambitious, and they have an above-average drive to make the best out of their learning opportunities. They have a relentless drive to be front and center where all the action takes place. Being a Front Row Seater means you have to come early because you have to put some effort and energy into scrambling for the highly prized front-row seats. There is thought and some strategy necessary for getting the best seat in the classroom.

Front Row Seaters Are Confident

Being where the teacher can see you means that you need to be fully prepared, because the teachers might be calling on you. Sitting close to the instructor also shows respect for his or her knowledge and efforts to teach you. Being a Front Row Seater also means that you need to take good care of yourself because you are conscious of making a good impression. Sitting in the front row means that you are confident with a healthy, strong self-esteem, as you are sitting in front of all the other students, subject to their critical eye as they notice everything you do.

Front Row Seaters Are Industrious

Being in the front rows is also a good reason to be a very good note taker: The instructor, teacher, or seminar leader easily notices the ambitious note-takers. From my own experience, the difference between the students who just sit there with no emotion on their faces and the students who are furiously taking notes is really noticeable! Your industriousness in taking notes will be thought about when leadership opportunities are discussed. You want to be noticed by your instructor in a positive way, because everyone needs letters of recommendation for getting into a school of higher learning, applying for financial scholarships, or for getting your dream job.

Front Row Seaters Have Better Social Skills

During a typical school week, there will be times when the teacher asks students to pair up for group work. This can be unsettling as students learn how to interact, take leadership roles, and work together to solve problems and then present their findings to the class. The quality of work from Front Row Seaters is noticeably of higher quality because of the higher social skills of Front Row Seaters. In the real world, these social skills translate to better employee participation in company-sponsored functions. But more importantly, your social skills as demonstrated by your class participation answer the employer's question about your ability to engage in productive business relationships and whether you can socialize effectively and entertain clients. Front Row Seaters generally are resourceful in developing great, powerful networking skills, which are invaluable to getting things done in the marketplace. From now on, make it a point to be a Front Row Seater! Scrambling to be front and center will be a leadership character trait that will be your ticket to greatness!

THE DOWNFALL OF THE BACK ROW SEATER

CAUTION! If you are a Back Row Seater, you may want to think twice about reading this next section. It might be too negative for you, but the reality is that most successful leaders will agree these thoughts are pretty representative of what does happen. Will these things happen if you always sit in the back row? Maybe not, but you need to understand all the ramifications of sitting in the back rows. Go ahead and read this section if you must, but then make it a point to be a Front Row Seater from now on!

Back Row Seaters Really Do Not Care

When Back Row Seaters look at the people sitting in the front rows, they are looking at their future bosses and future leaders. Back Row Seaters tend to treat life with casualness and a lack of self-respect. Back Row Seaters signal to the world that they really don't care. Back Row Seaters are mavericks and tend to be loners with weak social skills, which translates to a lifetime of broken relationships and financial frustration.

Back Row Seaters Are Content with Leftovers

Back Row Seaters: Do you realize that not only are you condemning your future but you are also condemning your children's future by where you sit? When you sit in the back row, you are establishing a pattern for life. You squash any ambition you have by settling for the leftover seats. ***Key Question:*** *"Where else in life do you settle for the leftovers?"*

Back Row Seaters Avoid Being Noticed

It takes no effort to get a back seat. You can come in late. You sit in the back where you will not be noticed. You have a good chance of avoiding being called on so you can get by with not being fully prepared for class. Sitting in the back row shows that you have no respect for the teacher. You can be sloppy in appearance because no one will notice you in the back row. Creating a great future for yourself is not in your plans, as you'd rather sit in the back row with your other party friends and goof off.

Back Row Seaters Tend Not to Show Up

Sitting in the back rows also means you can skip class without being noticed too much or at least you think you can—because, no matter how big the class, teachers generally know who is missing. When your ambition is to miss as many classes as you can get away with, you will also probably be an employee who will take advantage of all sick days possible. Missing work costs the marketplace billions of dollars each year in lost productivity. You never know when this employee will show up. They're not dependable and you can't really trust them.

Sitting in the back rows of a classroom establishes a pattern for life. You get used to taking a back seat to others ahead of you. Don't get used to the leftovers of life. Be a front row seater, always be first and get a jump start on life!

~Dr. Richard St. Germaine
University of Wisconsin, Eau Claire Campus

Back Row Seaters Have Bad Habits

As an employer, I am cautious in hiring Back Row Seaters because their back row attitude generally means they are pretty relaxed about taking care of themselves. It's a good assumption they are couch potatoes who watch a lot of TV, eat the worst food, and have an aversion to a healthy physical fitness program. Back Row Seaters may have addictive behaviors like alcoholism, smoking, and drug use. Depression caused by a lack of self-esteem is common amongst Back Row Seaters. It's almost a sure bet they will be a heavy hit on the company's health insurance!

Back Row Seaters Miss Out on Life's Opportunities

Back Row Seaters usually end up wondering how come the rewards of life pass them by. They get passed over for raises, promotions, and prime assignments that can lead to career-changing opportunities.

Intriguing Question: Ask yourself: Where else does this "Back Row Seater" mentality show up in my life and how has this held me back? How often have I sabotaged my own opportunities by not being noticed? How many times have I deliberately sought out the back rows? Who am I associating with in the back rows of life? Don't let your back row seating casualness turn you into one of life's casualties! From now on, start fighting to sit in the front rows. In fact, show your leadership skills: When you are sitting in a room and you notice everyone starting to fill up the back rows, see if you can challenge your classmates to join you in the front rows!

IMPORTANT: How Will Your Professors Remember You?

I want to leave you with a major thought: If *you* were the professor and you were asked to give a student your best recommendation for the job of their dreams, how would *you* think of *you* based on your appearance, attitude, behavior, and involvement in class? ***What you want on your job recommendation letter should be your guide on how you show up for class!***

COLLEGE SUCCESS TIPS: 8 Surefire Ways Your Leading Edge Difference Will Boost Your Success:

1. How You Show UP: Your appearance and attitude might be the Leading Edge Difference between a "B" and an "A."

2. The Leading Edge Difference will help build a relationship with your professor. Your professor will feel inclined to give you insights on how you can dramatically improve your papers and your test scores. If you respect professors in the classroom, they will go out of their way to help you.

3. The Leading Edge Difference will definitely help you get professors to recommend you for financial aid and scholarships.

4. The Leading Edge Difference will help get your professor to intervene with other professors when you need help getting into a class that is hard to get into!

5. The Leading Edge Difference will come in handy when getting a job on campus. A professor who is a raving fan of yours knows how to get their favorite student into the campus job market.

6. The Leading Edge Difference will come in handy when you need great recommendations for graduate school.

7. The Leading Edge Difference will be your best bet when you need great recommendations from your professors for the job of your dreams!

8. Sitting in the front rows will give you the Leading Edge Difference and make a lasting impression on your professors. From now on, be a Front Row Seater!

Isn't it interesting that when you walk into a movie theatre where it is dark and nobody notices you, you want to get the best seats in the house—front and center? Nobody wants to sit in the back rows. But in the classroom, where you are studying to create the life of your dreams and your parents are investing tens of thousands of hard-earned dollars, students scramble to sit in the back rows!

~Famous Dave Anderson
Founder of the World's Greatest BBQ Joint!

CHAPTER FOURTEEN

Kick Start Your Career By Interning and Working as an Apprentice

Jumpstart Your Career Through Internships or Apprenticeships
Before the Industrial Revolution, young people would indenture themselves to a master craftsman and work for free until they became proficient enough to go out on their own. They were apprentices, grateful just for the opportunity to learn their trade by working free for a master craftsman. Today, this is called *interning*. This is an excellent way to find out if your choice of careers is the right choice for you. It is highly recommended you begin internships even while you are still in high school.

On-the-Job Experience Will Give Greater Meaning to Your College Learning
The more you can work in a variety of jobs, the more likely you will be to find the career choice that's right for you. Also, being able to identify your career path will help you find relevance in your class work, which will make studying more meaningful for you. If you find a particular industry is not right for you, you still have plenty of time to intern with other companies. Your number-one goal should be to get as much experience as you can—and if that means offering your services for free, then it is a good trade-off for making the most important decision of your entire career.

The harder I work, the more I live.
George Bernard Shaw
Nobel Prize-Winning Author and Playwright

According to a Recent Career Builders* Survey of Employers...
The following college activities count as relevant work experience that you should list on your resume; ranked by popularity, these findings demonstrate why internships are so important:

- Internships — 62 percent
- Part-time jobs in another area or field — 50 percent
- Volunteer work — 40 percent
- Class work — 31 percent
- Involvement in school organizations — 23 percent
- Managing activities for sororities and fraternities — 21 percent
- Participation in sports — 13 percent

*For more great information on creating a rewarding career, check out www.careerbuilders.com

12 Reasons Why Internships Jumpstart Your Career

1. **Discover Your Career Choice.** You can experience firsthand if your career choice is right for you.

2. **Relevance for Course Work.** You quickly develop a sense of relevance, knowing why you are studying what you are studying. It makes your studies more meaningful and compels you to make the most of your education.

3. **How to Get Better Use Out of Your College Investment.** Interning may give you ideas for other coursework you that you may never would have thought of taking.

4. **Boss Can Help Give Direction In Your Studies.** Your internship employer may be able to help you with your course work, giving you practical insights into your research.

5. **Boss Can Help with Term Paper Ideas.** Your internship employer may even give you ideas for your term papers, regarding relevant subjects your industry is facing. Your employer may have some ideas that are more timely and relevant for your college research.

6. **Gaining "The Inside Track" In a Highly Competitive Job Market.** After you graduate, you will be able to hit the ground running. You won't be a newbie novice. You will have valuable work experience giving you great insights into the inner workings of your job.

7. **Learn the Industry Slang or Lingo.** Every industry has its own language. There are terms, industry jargon, and slang that reference or describe things specific to the industry. By interning, you become familiar with what people are referring to, and this helps when you are interviewing for a job. You won't look like a deer in the headlights in group conversations with company executives.

8. **You Can Gain Valuable Work Experience.** So when you graduate and a prospective employer asks you—"Do you have any experience?"—this won't frighten you!

9. **You May Be Creating a Future Job For Yourself.** Impressing your intern employer may create your first job opportunity!

10. **Valuable Networking Contacts.** Also, by working in the industry, you will be making valuable professional networking connections through the people you meet while interning. This is a great reason why you need to have your resume, Facebook, LinkedIn, and personal website ready.

11. **Great Job Recommendations and Building Your Industry Reputation.** You will be creating a solid reputation for your work ethic and building the basis for creating great job recommendations by your internship employers in case your desire is to go to a different geographical area.

12. **Get Involved In Your Industry and Business Community.** Join trade associations and the local chamber of commerce. Go to industry conferences and meet the movers and shakers within your industry. Joining the local chamber of commerce helps you meet movers and shakers within your community.

Make Good Use of the Campus Career Center for Getting Yourself Ready to Job Hunt

Get to know your campus career center immediately. This is an underused resource center that is dedicated to helping you find internships, a job, or the career of your dreams. The campus career center can help you craft your experiences into your best resume and, more importantly, they can help you with "mock interviews."

Great Advice: *Practice doing mock interviews!* The first time you get in front of an employer, you don't want to look like you've just seen a ghost. You'll be extremely grateful you practiced mock interviews in college. Don't downplay this—it could be the Slight Edge Difference that lands you the job of your dreams! GO FIND YOUR CAMPUS CAREER CENTER NOW!!! I am surprised how many students never take advantage of the services provided by this terrific resource.

Famous Dave's "Inside Secret": Get to know the career counselor early on and keep him or her updated on your progress. Holiday cards and thank-you notes will motivate the career counselor to put your name on the top of the short list with companies that have close relationships with your school!

Personality Tests

Some campus career centers will help you take personality tests so you know how to deal with these, as almost every worthwhile employer will ask you to take one as part of your interview process. Taking a personality test is great information to know about yourself and what it means to your employer.

Internships and Part-Time Job Opportunities

The career center is a great place to find information on internships and part-time job opportunities. The advisors at your campus career center can also help guide you in the art of job offers and salary negotiations. Get a head start and check all this out. Don't wait until you are ready to graduate. MAKE THIS YOUR GOAL: "My goal is to have several job offers before I get my diploma!" NOW WRITE IT DOWN!!!

Famous Dave's Insider Secrets to Getting Your Dream Internship!

Some universities or colleges have active internship programs. If your college has this option, great! And these ideas will help even with a structured internship program. If not, these ideas will help you create a surefire way to find your own internship opportunities! First, let's understand one thing: You may not get paid, or not much; but no matter how financially tough working for free may be for you, the real benefit is that you will be in the best position possible to land the job of your dreams upon graduation. During tough economic times, many employers have cut back on hiring anyone, much less an intern.

Famous Dave's Insider Secret to Getting Hired!

So here's some great advice that you will never see anywhere else! *The best way to get a job is NOT to formally ask to "intern."* When you ask for any internship openings, it may scare off any opportunities, because most bosses see interns as added responsibility, more paper work, and another expense. More responsibility to an already busy boss is not always appealing.

THIS IS THE CRITICAL IMPORTANT ADVICE: Your First Step... Is to Prime the Pump In Advance!

To make this work takes some thinking ahead. First, we start by adding some water to prime the pump (meaning you have to put something "in" before you get anything "out"). Almost six months before your summer break or when you would like to intern, start priming the pump. Identify half a dozen companies that best fit the career you would like to intern for, and research who the CEO, general manager, or head of human resources is for each company. Don't wait until you are ready to start interning to find this information out. You are developing great career skills, anticipating your next steps for achievement by being prepared in advance for any possible job opportunities.

Here's Famous Dave's Secret: Ask To Be Mentored!

Call or write a short note asking the CEO or GM to mentor you for a semester as part of your class assignment. Tell them that you are interested in choosing their industry as your career and that you would like to meet with them once a month for the next three or four months, for just 45 minutes each time so you can ask a few questions and allow them to give you any insights into what is happening in their industry. Almost every employer will be honored to do this. This will give you a foot in the door for asking later for an internship.

Send Your Future Employer Relevant Information to Show Your Interest In Their Company or Their Industry

Next, as you are doing your own research for class projects, I would also be Googling any relevant information that may impact a business within your field. Put yourself on Google Alert for any information that hits the news regarding this company. If the news is in a local newspaper, rush out and buy a copy. Cut out the article or copy it off you printer if you are downloading it from the Internet. Also, go a major bookstore and research any current trade magazines that may have some articles relevant to the business. Either buy the magazine or copy off something you find on the Internet and, with a nice note, send it to the CEO or GM.

Your note should read something like this: "Hi! My name is David Anderson. I am a student at the local University of Wisconsin and I am studying to be (your profession). I am familiar with your company, as you are a leader in our industry. I found this article while I was doing research for a class project and I just thought you might be interested in this information as well. Also, I wanted to congratulate you for all you do to make this country a great place to live"....or whatever you think is appropriate. Then, sign your name. I guarantee you that when you come to call on this person, the "The Doors Of Opportunity" will swing open faster than a hummingbird beats its wings!

Here's the Final Part of My Insider Secrets:

Just offer to work for free! But you have to know how to ask for the opportunity. Here's what you say" "Hi! My name is David Anderson. I am a student at the University of Wisconsin and I have some free time between classes. I am the type of person that always needs to stay busy. Look, you don't have to pay me, but I would love to have the opportunity to help you wherever I can—and I don't mind sweeping floors, running errands or anything I can do to make your life easier! I am a hard worker and extremely dependable. I promise I won't get in your way. I am an eager learner, I will be a big help to you, and the best part is that you don't have to pay me!"

"I am studying to enter your line of work and any real-world experience I can gain would be really helpful to me. I can start this afternoon—or would Monday morning be better for you?"

If your future internship employer says, "You're Hired!"—tell them you're excited to start and you're very honored to have this opportunity.

If You Don't Get Hired Right Away, Here's What You Do...

If the employer says, "I'll have to give your idea some consideration, but I'll get right back to you," you say: "That's great! Here's my resume and my contact information and I'll wait for your call!"

This is critical...

Next, you immediately write an appropriate thank you card to the employer, saying how much you enjoyed being mentored and that you look forward to the opportunity to help them make their company the best in the industry! And again, leave your contact information and the best time to call. You should leave this card with the employer's assistant the same day if possible, or they should get it in the mail the very next day. Best advice: Be prepared and carry the cards with you, ready to be filled out and dropped off in the mail.

This Famous Dave's Insider Secret Seals the Deal!

Now this is the important part... attach the thank you card to a token of your appreciation. Choose either a tin of gourmet popcorn, specialty cookies, chocolate-covered pretzels, or a pound of gourmet coffee. I don't think I would send chocolates unless you can't find something unique. The gourmet popcorn, specialty cookies, chocolate-covered pretzels, or gourmet coffee is fun and something that can be shared by everyone in the office—and this is your Leading Edge Difference, how you will be remembered! One more thing: Make sure you write another thank you card to the employer's executive assistant. This person will help you immensely in the future, once you have established a relationship.

I guarantee you no prospective student intern has used this introduction, you will definitely be considered, and you even have a good opportunity of getting paid handsomely, if you work your tail off and impress your employer. The ultimate upside is that you might have created your first job opportunity after graduation or the greatest job recommendation that you could ever hope for. More importantly, you will have created an industry friendly mentor or contact for life!

SUCCESS SKILLS 101: The Art of Executive Gift-Giving

To prime the pump or to show your appreciation, learning the art of executive gift-giving will be something extremely helpful that you will use the rest of your career! I recommend giving a gift of gourmet popcorn, specialty cookies, chocolate-covered pretzels, or a pound of gourmet coffee as simple thank you gifts. For a real big thank you or big congratulations on a big deal or a spectacular achievement. Whatever you send, make it distinctive by including a personal handwritten note.

My Own Personal Real World Internship Experience:
I Learned Valuable Life Lessons Worth Millions Because I Was
Willing to Work for Free!

I started my own business at age nineteen. I wholesaled planted dish gardens to retail florists. I learned the value of offering my hard work to other florists just so I could learn the tricks of the trade. Because of the excellent planted dish gardens I sold to my florists, I became good friends with a number of them; when I was done with my own work, I would go their shops and offer my help for free. I would sweep their floors, break down boxes, and even deliver flowers for them.

Many times, the florists offered to pay me partly because I often worked harder than their own employees! I never accepted their money, although it was tempting at times because I only had pennies in my pocket. However, the in-the-trenches, street-smart strategies I learned could have never been learned anywhere else. Here's the upside: Because I was such a hard worker, these florists told other florists about me and told them *they needed to buy* my dish gardens. When you freely help others, the paybacks are huge.

The skills I learned back then have helped all through my life. In return for me not accepting any money from them, they let me hang around while they created beautiful floral arrangements. I got to learn how they greeted their best customers. I learned invaluable lessons on how they negotiated pricing with their vendors. But most importantly, I gained their confidence, so I was able to ask them questions to help me make decisions in my own business. I have never regretted working for free because it was like I was investing in my reputation and my career. The life skills and career skills I learned working for free have been worth millions to me over my lifetime, much more than what I could have gotten if they paid me. I always share this example with high school and college students.

> *You know you are on the road to success if you would do*
> *your job, and not be paid for it.*

~Oprah Winfrey
America's Leading Television Host

Real-World Example of University of Minnesota Student Jena Barch's Internship Experience:

For the last ten years, I have been a mentor to a number of college students every year. When I started writing this section on interning, I asked my current mentee, Jena Barch, a student at The Carlson School of Business at The University of Minnesota, about her interning experience. Jena passionately spoke about how important it was for any college student to gain real-world experience in the industry they have chosen for their life's work, or even to find out if they are on the right track.

Here is a brief description of Jena's internships during her four years at the U of M. These are her own words:

- Carlson Wagonlit Travel: Paid, but would have done it gladly without pay!

- Greater Twin Cities United Way: Unpaid and I really wanted to do this for the experience of doing public relations for a non-profit, and I loved it!

- Paper Chase Litigation Technologies (a start-up company): Paid.

- Fallon Worldwide: Unpaid and I wanted the job desperately. (Jena explained the experience was very important to her to understand if this industry, advertising, was what she was looking for in a career.

Another Real World Example of Internship Success: Kris Shelton, From Internship to General Manager the Same Day as Graduation!

Here's another real good example of why it's so critical to have a driving desire to develop real-world experience as an intern while still in college. I have another mentee, Kris Shelton, who graduated from the University of Minnesota, Duluth Campus, in Business. Kris interned at our Famous Dave's Restaurant in Hayward, Wisconsin.

Kris is a remarkable young man who took a full course load while at the U of M, and worked full time his entire time at school. Challenging himself to burn the candle at both ends, Kris left school with relatively little debt compared to most students. Working for Famous Dave's, he also moved up the ladder before he even graduated and became Assistant Manager while still in his last year of college.

When Kris graduated, he was able to hit the ground running, as the same day he graduated from the University of Minnesota, we promoted him to General Manager. This was exciting for Kris, as many of his friends were having a tough time finding jobs in 2009, the height of one of the worst economic meltdowns in U.S. history. Kris avoided the angst that pained most of his friends looking for jobs in a very tough job market. In addition, Kris moved right into a higher-paying GM's position because of his years interning for Famous Dave's. It is rare for new college graduates to move into top positions at any company without paying their dues. This is another great example of why it's so important to intern during college!

Here's a Great Idea for Harvesting Internship Possibilities!

Join the local chamber of commerce or the trade association of your intended profession while you are in college. This is a great way for you to start cultivating your group social skills and start getting comfortable meeting the movers and shakers of your community. You will have an opportunity to meet key executives or owners of companies. When you attend your local chamber of commerce meeting, introduce yourself as a student at the local university or college. All the key movers and shakers in town will introduce themselves to you and now you have introductions to possible jobs and internships! Going to your local chamber of commerce meetings or trade association meetings is the best way to get your foot in the door of local businesses as well as getting to know many of the fine community organizations that are members.

CHAPTER FIFTEEN

POWERHOUSE NETWORKING

It's Not Who You Know But It's All About Who Knows What You Know About THEM!

Getting Involved On Campus Helps Develop Your Social Skills and Networking Skills...PLUS, I Share One of My Best "Inside Secrets!"
Two of the most important career skills that will dramatically improve your chances for success are your networking and your relationship skills. You can be the most talented, hard-working, and skilled employee, but if no one knows about you, you will live an obscure, average life! I cannot emphasize enough how important it is to get involved in campus organizations to develop your networking and relationship skills. I also highly recommend joining community organizations where leaders of your local community are actively involved. One of the benefits of getting involved in your community is that you have unlimited access to some of the top business leaders, community organizers, and entrepreneurs during these local get-togethers.

Here's one of my best **Famous Dave's "Inside Secrets":** Volunteer to help organize the meetings and help pass out name tags. When members check in for the meetings, make sure you get to be the one who greets everyone when they arrive. Look sharp and radiate the biggest glowing smile you've got! This important "inside secret" will get you on a first-name basis with every influential member in your community. Very powerful stuff!

Joining My Local Chamber of Commerce Helped Jumpstart My Business Career

Early in my business career, I had a business owner who took me under his wing and was a great mentor. He suggested that if I really wanted to jumpstart my career and meet all the right people, it would be highly beneficial to join the local chamber of commerce. I took his advice and, to my wonderful enlightenment, I found out that the loan officers of banks do not attend the chamber of commerce meetings—it's the presidents of the banks that show up! Because I never missed a meeting and I always volunteered to help out, I got to know the president of our local bank, Gerhardt Umlauf. Gary grew to like me, and my first business loan in 1973 was for $10,000 dollars just on my signature alone! And back then, $10,000 was a lot of money! Here's an interesting question: "If I had gone directly to the bank, how easy do you think it would have been for me to get past the loan officers and ask to see the president of the bank?"

The Power of Your ADDRESS BOOK

One valuable tool to developing your lifetime network of resources is your address book. I not only have an address book on my smart phone, I also have a paper-bound address book, a computer address book, and a three-ring binder of plastic sheaves where I keep business cards. *Don't even think of starting college without having an address book!* Get into the habit of asking for people's full contact information even while you are in college. Once you are on the job, asking people for their full contact information will be second nature to you. Success is not only about relationships but it is also about your connections, your resources, and the relationships you cultivate by staying in touch.

> *More business decisions occur over lunch and dinner than at any other time, yet no MBA courses are given on the subject.*
>
> ~Peter Drucker
> High-Level Management Consultant and Business Writer

Create a Gold Mine of Email Contacts

Your email address file should be considered a gold mine of resources and contacts. Keep these contacts informed by developing your own quarterly updates of what you are up to and include useful, profound tidbits of information. When you send out updates, make use of any current pictures you have of yourself. The more you can put your face in front of the world, the greater your Personal Brand becomes recognized.

> *Information technology and business are becoming inextricably interwoven. I don't think anybody can talk meaningfully about one without talking about the other.*
>
> ~Bill Gates
> Founder, Microsoft

Unleash the Networking Power of Your Business Card

Everything you do should be geared to separating yourself from the masses—this includes even your business card! Everyone, even students in school, have business cards, but most keep them hidden in their wallets or purse. Use your business card to give you a competitive edge and turn this little piece of paper into a global networking powerhouse. Paper the universe with your business card. Get used to handing it out and making influential business contacts. One of the most important paybacks of handing out your business card is getting one back. BUT it's not the card you're after, it's the email address.

Awesome Ideas On How to Turn Your Business Card Into a "Cash Cow" Networking Powerhouse!

- Put your email address, personal website, Facebook, Twitter, and LinkedIn addresses on your card.
- Use the back of your card for promotional information about yourself.
- Use a great quote that best represents you.
- List any awards or recognition you have won.

- Provide a little-known industry secret that will create an "aha moment" for the reader. (Something interesting about your industry can be found via Google)
- Put something funny that's memorable on the back of the card, if appropriate!
- Don't be tempted to self-print your cards on your home printer. Be professional and get your cards done right.
- Find someone in your school who is a graphic arts major and get them to design your card.
- Use a logo. If you don't have an idea, just use your initials and place them on top or under a symbol of the profession you are interested in. You can get the symbol off the Internet.
- Don't use cheap paper. For a couple of bucks more, you can have a card that is a WOW!

Create a Job Title for Your Business Card That Will Unlock Doors!

You may be a student without a job title, but you can still turn your business card into a networking powerhouse: Just call yourself a "Researcher"! Since you are a student, there is a lot of truth to that title, but it will also allow you to ask information-gathering questions or even schedule hard-to-get appointments. For example: If you are a medical student, you can title yourself "Medical Researcher"; law student, "Legal Researcher"; architecture student, "Architectural Researcher"; marketing student, "Market Researcher"!

The Successful follow their dreams. The Average follow their job descriptions.

~Famous Dave Anderson
Founder of the World's Greatest BBQ Joint!

SUCCESS SKILLS 101: Harvesting a Wealth of Internet Resources From Your Email List.

The digital universe is a wealth of untapped resources. Today, a business card not only contains an email address but may also have a website listed. Bookmark key websites on your computer. They are instant gold mines for harvesting key information that helps you develop your "Intellectual Capital." Your email address file, over time, will become an unlimited gold mine from which you can harvest key contacts, sales leads, and an important source of industry information. Here's a great success tip: Google "The Harvey MacKay 66." Harvey MacKay is the founder of MacKay Envelope and a *New York Times* bestselling author and highly requested keynote speaker. Harvey provides 66 key questions to be answered about important contacts you meet. These 66 questions give you a great outline for discovering the most critical information you should know about your customers or key people in your life. Check this out!

The successful networkers I know, the ones receiving tons of referrals and feeling truly happy about themselves, continually put the other person's needs ahead of their own.

~Bob Burg
Successful Author On Networking

CHAPTER SIXTEEN

Don't Expect Success
If You Haven't Studied Success!

Here's an interesting question: "Have you studied Success? Have you ever taken a course called Success 101?" If your answer is NO, then the next real interesting question is: "If you've never seriously studied Success, how do you expect to become successful?"

Don't go to college with the intention just to get good grades, a diploma, or a job. Go to college with the intention that you are going to study "How to Become Successful!" The study of success is just as important as anything you will study in college. The study of success helps you develop an unwavering, optimistic ATTITUDE needed to take on the toughest challenges of life. College is supposed to prepare you to be someone who can lead organizations, businesses, or teams to greater heights of achievement, productivity, and profitability. But are you really studying this? Take a look at your courses: Is success the eventual outcome? Do you really know what it takes to become very successful in life?

Leadership Quiz: Think of people you know who are real winners and leaders in life. Now think about what words best describe these people.

Whenever I do this Leadership Exercise with a class of students or a team of executives in business, the answers are pretty much the same when describing the winning characteristics of someone they respect as a leader or a champion.

Here are some of the most common descriptive words I get back as answers for describing Successful People, Achievers, Entrepreneurs, Superstars, Champions, and Respected Leaders:

Determined	Persistent	Caring
Loving	Goal-Driven	Generous
Cheerful	Healthy	Ambitious
Loyal	Trustworthy	Honest
Dependable	Passionate	Volunteers
Optimistic	Enthusiastic	Disciplined
Work Ethic	Achiever	Leadership
Motivated	Excellence	Inspiring
Fun-Loving	Communicator	Creative
Team Player	Well-Groomed	Talented
Selfless	Giver	Winner
Hard Worker	Spiritual	Self-Starter
Energetic	Attentive	Positive
Confident	Friendly	Upbeat

If these are the most common words used to describe winners and leaders in life, how many of these words describe you? How many of these words are character traits you will be studying college?

Next, ask yourself: "How many of these words are ATTITUDE or SKILLS?" Go over this list and put an "A" for "attitude" or an "S" for "skill" next to the above words that best describe these character traits. You will find that almost all of the words are descriptive of *attitude*! *Skills* and *disciplines* to develop your APTITUDE are taught in school. Make sure you read this as *aptitude*. Aptitude is the responsibility of your schooling. Attitude is your responsibility.

Success is determined by your attitude, which is something you have to choose every day you get up. It is up to you to develop your *attitude* and it is up to your professors to teach you the technical skills you will need to succeed in your career. Just remember: *Your attitude comes from you and it is your choice.*

This Book Will Reveal the Success Strategies You Need to Master While In College!
As you read this book, develop the attitude that no matter how these strategies or success tips may seem out of your comfort zone, make up your mind that you are going to overcome any hesitation to go full out to learn these College Success Strategies. Mastering these strategies will give you the jumpstart in life that you deserve! Now that you know what employers are looking for, what character traits do you think your professors would use to describe you? And then, consistently, throughout your four years in college, work to be the best role model for these character traits.

> *The winner's edge is not in a gifted birth, a high IQ, or in talent. The winner's edge is all in the attitude, not aptitude. Attitude is the criterion for success.*
> ~Denis Waitley
> Performance Expert and Author

SUCCESS SKILLS 101: Personal Research and Development. College is only a small part of your life's education. A lifelong personal commitment to growth and development is essential to your success in life and in your career. Identify growth areas in your life you need to work on. These may include: persuasive public speaking, the art of selling, financial literacy, business etiquette, health and nutrition, physical fitness, networking skills, personal public relations and self promotion, and keeping technologically updated and relevant. Go to seminars that challenge, transform, and stretch you. Get involved in your industry trade associations. Find a successful industry mentor and apprentice yourself to this person. Start building your Success Library. Start listening to inspiring audio books every time you get into your car!

CHAPTER SEVENTEEN

Personal Research and Development and Understanding "The Four Career Knowledge Areas" of Intellectual Capital

Personal Research and Development: Knowing the Four "Career Knowledge Areas" That Develop Intellectual Capital for Your Career Will Help You Create Your College Development Plan. THIS IS CRITICAL STUFF—MAKE SURE YOU GET THIS!!!

As you go through college, you should group your learning experiences into the four types of career knowledge you will need in the real world. I am amazed that college graduates are not cognizant of how their careers; *Intellectual Capital* is created. Intellectual capital is basically your valuable insights and experience, knowing how to be highly productive, create value, and be profitable in your industry. Your value to the marketplace will be valued by the depth of your Intellectual Capital experience.

Graduates show up ready to go to work, but they often don't have their own plan of what they need to learn—which is really a defined lifelong plan of personal research and development. Understanding these four areas of Intellectual Capital will jumpstart your career. This is another one of Famous Dave Anderson's profound gems of wisdom because you'll never hear it explained like this anywhere else! In fact, share this information on Intellectual Capital with your classmates, it will be greatly beneficial to their success as well!

Your Career Knowledge or "Intellectual Capital" should be categorized into *Four Career Knowledge Areas* that will make up your own lifelong Personal Research and Development Program:

1. **How to "Do Your Job" Knowledge**
   - The ins and outs of being highly productive at your job.
   - Being up-to-date on technology.
   - Developing the expertise to be best-in-class or achieving the recognition of being a highly trained professional.
   - Personal ambition to add something new to your resume every six months.
   - Knowing how your job creates profits.
   - Obsessive devotion to serving customers.
   - Developing great relationships with co-workers.
   - Being able to train others do a better job.

2. **How to "Get Stuff Done Within Your Company" Knowledge**
   - Knowing the history of your company.
   - Knowing who does what inside your company.
   - Thorough knowledge of policies and procedures.
   - Knowing how to get stuff done inside your company.
   - Possessing enthusiastic team spirit and being a raving, loyal ambassador.

3. **Knowing "What's Going On Within Your Industry" Knowledge**
   - Knowing who your competitors are and knowing their strengths and weaknesses.
   - Knowledge of possible new customers.
   - Keeping updated with new trends, innovations, new products, and the latest technologies.
   - Knowing the movers and shakers in your industry on a personal-name basis.
   - Joining and participating in trade associations.

- Supporting your industry by sharing your expertise at trade conventions.
- Submitting articles to trade journals.

4. "Developing Your Own Personal Success" Knowledge

- Reading inspiring books on management, leadership, and success.
- Investing in self-improvement seminars and classes.
- Improving your skills to speak in public.
- Learning how to sell and influence buyers.
- Knowing how to invest your earnings and develop an investment portfolio.
- Health and nutrition knowledge.
- Staying technologically updated and relevant.
- Learning how to teach and train—expanding your influence.

A lifelong commitment to a Personal Research and Development Program will be the foundation for creating your Intellectual Capital. Intellectual Capital is based on your productivity, creativeness, leadership, and profitability. This creates your value within the marketplace, and is also vital to your Personal Branding.

~James W. Anderson
Entrepreneur, Speaker, and Author

SUCCESS SKILLS 101: Create Value Everyday of Your Life
Everything you learn should be learned for the purposes of creating value into the lives of other people and for making the world a better place. This is also called PROFIT. Profit is nothing more than creating value. Give beyond expectation in everything you do. When you create more value than you are paid—this is how abundance is created. Everyday produce more than you consume. Never consume more than you produce. Your ability to create value or abundance is how the marketplace values your "Intellectual Capital." When you can understand how everything you learn can be used to create value or abundance into the lives of others—you will have discovered the true purpose of education!

Your College Education and Experience On Campus Begins Building Your Intellectual Capital.
Think about how you can start building while in college your career's Intellectual Capital using the Four Career Knowledge Areas. Knowing how your career Intellectual Capital is created will help you create a similar understanding of how your college education should be structured in your mind. Start cultivating a mindset that your career's lifelong commitment to Personal Research and Development is nothing more than an extension of your college education. Yes, you heard right: If you understand what I am saying here, you'll understand that I am making an argument that if you think you are studying hard now, it isn't going to end. You will be studying even harder after college just to keep up and stay relevant!

Lifelong Learning Is Now the New Paradigm Shift
We are living in new times. Our parents were able to stretch their one-time education over a whole career. Today, that is no longer possible. *We are living in an unprecedented accelerated changing times where what you learn today may be outdated by tomorrow!*

So it's important to develop the mindset right from the beginning of your college education: *How you are going to start developing your intellectual capital that makes you valuable to whatever the current needs are of the marketplace?*

1. **The college version of "knowing how to do your job" is the same as "knowing how to succeed in getting good grades."**
    - Knowing how to succeed in classroom skills.
    - Knowing how to meet the requirements and gain winning approval of your professors.
    - Knowing best practices for study and test-taking.
    - Getting involved in a study group to develop relationship skills.
    - Being up-to-date on technology.

2. **The college version of "knowing how to get stuff done within your company" is the same as "knowing how to get stuff done within your college campus."**
   - Knowing where all the key buildings are on campus.
   - Knowing the ins and outs of getting things done on campus.
   - Knowing how to access campus resources.
   - Getting involved in on-campus activities.
   - Team spirit: Knowing what's happening with your sports teams, debate teams, etc.
   - Being a raving, loyal ambassador for your school.

3. **Knowing "Industry Knowledge" is the same for college. Get involved in your future industry as if you were already on the job.**
   - Knowing the movers and shakers in your industry.
   - Supporting your industry by being knowledgeable.
   - Joining on-campus industry clubs if available.
   - Joining local trade associations.
   - Going to industry trade conventions.

4. **"Developing your own Success Knowledge" is the same for college as for your career's Success Knowledge. Start studying success as if you were already on the job.**
   - Reading inspiring books on management, leadership, and success.
   - Investing in self-improvement seminars and classes.
   - Improving your skills to speak in public.
   - Learning how to sell and influence buyers.
   - Knowing how to invest your earnings and develop an investment portfolio.
   - Paying attention to your health and nutrition.
   - Staying technologically updated and relevant.
   - Learning how to teach and train—expanding your influence.

Cultivate a lifelong commitment to Personal Research and Development while in college and understand the four levels of how to develop your career's Intellectual Capital

Apply this to your college experience and you will have gained an enormous head start in creating a successful and rewarding career. There is incredible brilliance and deep meaning in the following quote (especially the part I've underlined). Make sure you understand it. If not, reread and reread it until you grasp it with total comprehension!

> *Don't bring your need to the marketplace, bring your skill. If you don't feel well, tell your doctor, but not the marketplace. If you need money, go to the bank, but not the marketplace.*
>
> ~Jim Rohn
> America's Foremost Business Philosopher

Developing Your Intellectual Capital While In College

Here's some great advice: As soon as you find your career choice, subscribe to your industry's trade journals. In these trade magazines, you will find updates on latest trends and editorials by top industry thought leaders; find out what movers and shakers are getting promoted; learn about innovations and new products, marketing ideas, industry financing information, important news on legal and government regulations, industry economic trends; see ads by top industry companies; read news on upcoming trade conventions, and upcoming industry keynote speakers; and, most importantly, you'll find ads by leading industry headhunters and company job announcements! Make sure you go to industry conferences and pass out your business card; this is how you start building your Personal Brand.

Next, as you go through these trade journals, start bookmarking all the websites. When you have time from your studies, research these websites. Explore each company's website and make notes of anything interesting that makes these websites stand out or anything they proudly display.

Most companies have a section on their corporate culture, so check it out. You'll also want to check out its leadership or employee webpage to see what they're saying about career opportunities at this company. Look at the press releases and media section of the website to see why the company has been in the news. By the time you start sending out resumes, you'll have a great head start in knowing "inside stuff" about your future career!

Make it your goal to become a person of influence within your industry or profession by developing a solid research base of information. Your Intellectual Capital should be accurate, up-to-date, relevant, and second to none!

Man's mind, once stretched by a new idea, never regains its original dimensions.

~Oliver Wendell Holmes
American Jurist, Author, and Supreme Court Justice

CHAPTER EIGHTEEN

Do You Want to Know...
the Greatest Secret to Success
In College, Your Career, and In Life?

The Answer Will Shock You!

HERE'S THE BIG SECRET WHY YOU ARE REALLY IN COLLEGE!
Remember when your parents were nagging on you throughout your K-12 years to "study hard because you are going to college?" You probably imagined going to college was just about four more years of listening to professors and doing a lot of reading, research, and writing papers just to get a degree. WRONG, WRONG, WRONG!!!!

College Probably Should Be Renamed: PROBLEMS 101 UNIVERSITY. *The number one reason, you are in college is to better prepare yourself for being able to deal with life's greatest gift: PROBLEMS and ADVERSITIES!!!*

WOW! You never thought you were going to college to learn how to deal with gut-wrenching problems that wreak havoc on your life!

Want to know my BIGGEST SECRET WISH? I wish my parents and teachers would have done a better job in teaching me that life after school wasn't going to be about singing "Kum Ba Yah" around a campfire; but life was going to be about dealing with tormenting problems, tough challenges, and seemingly impossible adversities!

Yes, Life at Times Sucks...GET OVER IT!!!!
Welcome to life! Yes, life sucks sometimes and maybe all the time. Life is not fair. There are things that happen in life that just don't make sense. Stuff happens. And get this through your head: No one is picking on you! When life just doesn't seem fair, think of it this way: *There would be no opportunities for you if life was fair!*

Great Leaders Are Forged Through Adversity
The fact is, problems and adversities forge your character. Leaders could never become great leaders without being able to lead their followers through life's challenges. Think of every great leader in any profession and you will find a history of having to overcome some incredible adversity.

See Problems In a Good Way
Problems should jumpstart your adrenaline and get you motivated just like a good football game against a tough challenging team who is trying to crush you. In football, you know you are going up against a tough opponent, but you anticipate the challenge with optimism and team spirit! This should be the mindset of all the challenges you face. Don't fear problems and adversities, but look forward to them as opportunities for you to prove that you are a winner!

You Grow Through Life's Toughest Challenges
Problems should not get you down. Problems should not defeat you. You are blessed with problems so you can grow and test yourself to see how brilliant you are and to see what you are really capable of achieving. Problems should jumpstart your creativity!

Your problems should never become your excuses.
~Famous Dave Anderson
Founder of the World's Greatest BBQ Joint!

You Are Not Being Singled Out—Everyone Has Huge Problems
Remember this: Everyone has problems. All successful people have their own stories how they overcame their greatest adversity. You too will get through your tough times. Just keep repeating to yourself: This too shall pass, this too shall pass. Tomorrow will be a fresh start! Nothing can get me down. I will survive and I will come back stronger and wiser!

> *A setback is nothing but a setup for a comeback!*
> ~Willie Jolley
> Electrifying Motivational Speaker

Step Up and Take Responsibility for Resolving Problems
College is all about learning how to take care of yourself. "Taking care of yourself" is not just about getting to school on time, studying, or doing research. College is about learning how to think so you can function when you are faced with life's crushing problems. Most people live frustrated lives and never accomplish anything because they have run from problems all their lives. They are blameful because they cannot step up and take responsibility for handling their share of the problems. Your life will change immensely once you start stepping up and start taking responsibility for tackling the problems everyone else is running from!

The greatest opportunities come from the toughest adversities that are hair-pulling, depressing, gut-wrenching, and might make you wish that you were never born. Great leaders, business leaders, great parents, and great coaches are all adept at resolving problems for themselves, for the team, and for society. Leaders don't melt under adversities. In this book, I make a good argument for learning strategies on how to get better grades and how to enjoy your college experience; but if there is anything meaningful you learn from this book, it is to learn how you can successfully function while under the stress of life's greatest adversities. Your ability to take on life's tough challenges will be your most valuable asset to your future employer! When you can learn how to do this, the world will be beating a path to your doorstep!

All Through Life You Will Have Tough Competition and Challenging Opponents

Sports is about competing against tough competitors who have one goal—and that is to defeat you and crush you. In life, you will be competing against tough business competitors who want to crush you out of business. Maybe you will be a community activist or political leader who is going against mainstream opinions and you are fighting to turn them around to your way of thinking. The same inspiring team spirit and unwavering belief that motivates you and your team against another team that is trying with every last ounce of energy to crush your team, is the spirit used to take on life's adversities. Don't ever give up. Re-energize your spirit and move onward and upward!

The Quality of the Person You Become Will Mirror the Quality of the Challenges You Face or the Quality of Your Opponents

Remember this: The greater you are, the greater your adversaries! Your toughness, leadership, and
greatness will be reflected by the quality of people trying to oppose you. Think of it this way: The best championship games to watch are the ones where you have the best of the best trying to defeat each other. Be worthy of great competitors! But most importantly: *Give your adversaries the game of their lives!* Yes, you may feel whipped, but make sure your adversaries knows they were in one hell of a tough battle, too!

> *I have learned that success is to be measured not so much by the position that one has reached in life as by the obstacles which he has overcome.*
>
> ~Booker T. Washington
> America's Foremost Black Educator

You Have Arrived When You Can Tell the World: "Give Me Your Problems! I'll Help You!"

Step up and tell the world that you will handle its problems. Tell the world that they can trust you because you love problems. You love challenges and you don't buckle under pressure. If you understand that all opportunity comes from adversity, then you will also know that opportunities are virtually unlimited!

Don't Go It Alone—Get Help When You Need It

The most important thing to remember about problems is that everyone has been there before. Don't go it alone. Get help when you do feel you are having a tough time. If you ever feel like you are falling behind in your work, get help immediately. Talk to your advisor or your professor. They have helped many students over the years. Call home. You will get through your challenges. Just hang in there. Remember this: No one can defeat you unless you give them permission!

> *No one can make you feel inferior without your consent.*
> ~Eleanor Roosevelt
> First Lady, Wife of President Franklin Delano Roosevelt

Take Good Care of Your Emotional Health

College can be emotionally draining. From day one, you are under pressure knowing you have to make the most out of college because you are setting yourself up for the rest of your life. Your parents have put pressure on you to succeed because they are working their tails off to pay for your tuition. Today, with a depressed economy, the stress of studying for four years, and then not being sure you can even find a job has caused elevated levels of stress. Thoughts of suicide are a very real danger in college life today—it's something you can't take too lightly.

Know the symptoms of depression:

- Decreased energy, fatigue.
- Sadness, empty feelings, feeling lost.
- Loss of interest in normal activities.
- Inability to sleep.
- Feelings of hopelessness or worthlessness.
- Difficulty concentrating, making decisions.

Don't Be Above Getting Help Immediately

If you recognize any of these symptoms, get help immediately. Don't let your worries drive you sick. Go to the campus health center or speak to your advisor. Just share your feelings and, most importantly, don't feel like you need to hide these feelings. You are not the only one that has felt this way! Striking out into the real world alone can be a traumatic experience. You will get over it, but don't feel you have to do this alone. You will start to feel at ease once you can share your thoughts with someone who can help you. Remember that everyone wants you to succeed.

You Can Keep Yourself From Getting Depressed

Yes, college can be tough. However, feeling depressed is like deliberately running yourself through a gauntlet of battering rams. Most of our lousy feelings come from what we listen to in our own minds. We do this to ourselves for no good reason. When this happens, immediately go to your goals and your Vision Book to remind yourself of all the positive things in your life and all the things you need to be thankful for. This will help.

Keep this in mind. You are in control of your emotions by what you feed into your mind. Practice positive self-talk and positive reinforcing of the mind by controlling what you will let influence you. Always stay optimistic about your future, no matter how tough some days may seem. Stack the deck in your favor by avoiding negative people and negative stuff. Don't watch negative news on TV or read negative stuff in newspapers. Don't go to movies that will depress you. Don't watch scary stuff that will give you nightmares. Get rid of all the toxic influences in your life. *Don't fill your beautiful mind with trash!*

Your Mind Is Precious: Only Put Good Stuff In It—No Garbage!

One of the world's foremost experts on personal development, Zig Ziglar, encourages folks to put *the pure, the clean, the positive, and the powerful* into your mind! Don't let other people fill your head with gossip or trash talk. Read positive, inspiring books. Participate in stimulating, challenging group activities and sports, and practice having fun with positive people who love life.

PROBLEMS 101: Dealing With Adversities.
Decide in advance how you will deal with life's disappointments and gut-wrenching adversities when they happen—and they will happen, so it's best to be prepared. Will problems get you down or will they inspire you? In your Vision Book, write down your Action Plan for Adversities. Repeat positive affirmations over and over again in your head. Listen to positive, uplifting songs, motivational messages from audio books downloaded on your MP3 player. Place uplifting success quotes around your room. Get with friends who make you laugh. Seek help immediately from one of your advisors. Call home. Just knowing you have a Positive Plan of Action will keep you from turning into a sniveling ball of protoplasm the first time your world crashes!

Take Care of Your Health to Stay Energized!

A huge part of not getting depressed and keeping a positive, optimistic, cheerful mind is to stay healthy. Stay in shape and eat vegetarian as much as possible. (Except when you splurge and you just have to go out and get some of Famous Dave's great-tasting ribs! This is always a positive uplifting experience!) Stay away from junk foods to get off the roller coaster effect of emotional highs and lows. *Stay away from fast foods as much as possible.* Eating greasy foods causes your blood to become sluggish, and too many carbs from drinking sugary soda pops will cause sugar rushes and deep crashes, causing you to feel tired and emotionally drained. Drink water, water, water. Drink a glass of water when you wake up. Drink a glass of water before you eat breakfast, a glass of water mid-morning, a glass of water before you eat lunch, a glass of water mid-afternoon, a glass of water when you get back to your dorm, and a glass of water before your dinner. Water helps wash out toxins and helps keeps your blood refreshed—and you feeling energized!

A gem cannot be polished without friction,
nor a man perfected without trials.
~Chinese Proverb

There's a Good Reason to Make Your Bed Every Morning!
The first thing you do after getting out of bed is to make your bed. This starts your day out right. Start cultivating simple daily disciplines in college that become an integral part of your success habits throughout your life. Make your bed without fail. Making your bed needs to be the first thing you do before you get dressed. Your bed is the biggest thing in your room. Having a well-made bed will give you a good feeling walking back into your room. When you've had a crappy day and you've just walked into your room, having a clean, neat, welcoming room will help adjust your attitude. But if you had a crappy day and you came back to a sloppy, messy room, your room could actually add more fuel to how lousy you feel. If you don't know how to make your bed, LEARN! You can learn how to make your bed on YouTube. Hang up your clothes. Clean up your mess! Having a clean room makes a huge difference to your attitude and your emotional health.

When you're having a tough day, remember this great advice from one of America's Internet giants...

> *With regard to whatever worries you, not only accept the worst thing that could happen, but make it a point to quantify what the worst thing could be. Very seldom will the worst consequence be anywhere near as bad as a cloud of "undefined consequences." My father would tell me early on, when I was struggling and losing my shirt trying to get Parsons Technology going, "Well, Robert, if it doesn't work, they can't eat you!"*

~Robert Parsons
Founder of GoDaddy.com

SUCCESS SKILLS 101: Make Your Environment a Positive One. Surround Yourself With Positive Affirmations!
Keep a list of great ideas, inspiring sayings, and positive affirmations, and place these all around you. Keep positive, inspiring sayings in your notebook. Memorize the best inspiring, uplifting success quotes and constantly repeat them over and over again to yourself throughout the day. Write encouraging, uplifting quotes on Post-it Notes and place them on your mirror, in your locker, in your car. Frame your best thoughts and hang them on your wall. The more you can power up your mind with positive affirmations, the easier it will be to be impervious to the naysayers around you and all the negativity in the world. Instead, you will focus on being a good finder. You will see only the best in others. You will see opportunity in adversity. You will be *solution conscious*, NOT problem conscious. You will be in control of your own destiny! Things always get better and life goes on!

Thousands of candles can be lighted from a single candle, and the life of the candle will not be shortened. Happiness never decreases by being shared!

~Buddha

Famous Dave's "Insider Secret!": *Never lose hope!* The key to all my success has been to never give up hope when I was facing my darkest hour and all seemed hopeless. My compelling purpose to always take care of my family has driven me relentlessly to overcome all adversity. I have learned there is always a solution if you handle adversity with optimism, not fear. The most important thing is to always believe in yourself and never, ever give up on your dreams!

CHAPTER NINETEEN

Financial Literacy

"Show Me the Money!"
~ Rod Tidwell (Cuba Gooding Jr.), in the film *Jerry Maguire*

Learn How to Be Financially Self-Sufficient
I think one of greatest tragedies of our time is not making Financial Literacy a mandatory college course, or even a mandatory high school course. When I talk about financial literacy, I am not talking about accounting. I am talking about "How to Build a Personal Portfolio of Investments." Most people go through life just making ends meet and living from paycheck to paycheck. It is almost a tragedy to turn college students loose into the real world without knowing how to create a budget. *Turning in a weekly budget should be mandatory, just like homework!*

Does Your School Teach You How to Start Building an Investment Portfolio?
America's whole economy is based on the free enterprise system of capitalism, which is fueled by the savings and investment of the average American! Here's the problem: If this system's foundation is based upon the investment capacity of the average American, why aren't we teaching our youth how to start building investment portfolios? As a student starting out in life, one of your life's goals should be to *achieve financial independence.* Make it your personal goal to be as financially literate as you can be. Financial literacy should be studied with the same intensity as any course you take for your major!

Students Severely Underestimate the True Cost of College!

One of the biggest problems for newbies in college is severely underestimating the cost of going to college. You can't raid your mom's purse anymore. You are alone now, having to make financial decisions like a grownup! One of the most important daily habits you can master living on your own is how to budget your money. Before you leave home, thoroughly think through how every penny is going to be spent of the money you are bringing to college.

Create a "realistic" budget, considering the following:

Tuition
Room and board
Books
Student fees
Activity fees
Joining a fraternity or a sorority costs
Possible tutoring
Office and filing supplies
Copying costs
Quality computer with the right software and quality printer costs (printer ink and paper)
Postage and quality paper and envelopes for sending out resumes
Groceries
Coffee or Starbucks (almost as expensive as drinking!)
Snacks
Eating out with friends
Date night money
Spending money
Parking meter money
Parking fees and tickets (schools are notorious for ticketing cars parked where they shouldn't be parked or meters not fed)
Cell phone and monthly charges (this can get out of hand)
Emergency money
Urgent Care (falling out of the balcony of your girlfriend's dorm room—you'd be surprised!)

Initial Fixing Up Dorm Room
Clothes
Set of nice dress Clothes for interning and interviews
Decent briefcase for interning and interviews
Backpack for books
Party money (here's another area that can trip you up)
Cigarettes (hopefully this is not a line item for you)
Gas money (cars not recommended first year, but you need to pitch in if you are going anywhere with a friend who has a car)
Travel money (going home once in awhile)
Spring break travel
Travel money for job interviews
Travel money to attend industry conferences (job prospecting and developing industry Intellectual Capital)
Graduation costs
Moving back home expense or moving to new job location

Financial Management Is One of the Most Critical Life Skills You Can Develop for Your Career and Your Personal Life!
Managing your money is just as important as any college class you will take. If your college has any type of financial literacy course, make sure you take it! Set up a checking account and learn how to balance your checkbook. Keep your checkbook balanced at all times. How you manage your financial affairs in college will be very telling of how you will manage your financial affairs in your career and in all areas of your life. Get into the habit of knowing where every penny of your money is at all times! Your biggest headaches in life will come from having no money! Many careers have been ruined because of poor money skills. One of biggest causes of divorce comes from families having money problems and parents fighting over money.

In order to manage your money, get into the habit of asking for a receipt for EVERYTHING when you spend money. Keep a spiral-bound notebook with pocket folders to keep your receipts from your spending so you know how every single penny of your money was spent.

Identify your spending by the previous mentioned budget categories. Or create an Excel spreadsheet on your computer, which is probably better than a spiral-bound notebook. But the lesson is: *Keep track of your money!* The spending history you create will be helpful in planning next year's budget.

Abolish the Use of Credit Cards

Credit cards can doom you to a life of debt. Don't use them unless absolutely necessary. Use a debit card instead. If your parents give you a credit card, lock it up safe and secure. Don't use it just because they gave it to you. The interest rates on credit cards will eat you up, if you don't pay them off completely each month. Compounded interest on credit cards is evil.

It's Critical to Discuss Your Finances and How You Are Doing In School With Your Parents

Just as important as money management is having the maturity to talk openly with your parents about how you are doing financially and how everything else is shaping up for you in college. It is all part of being responsible and it gets you in the habit of talking dollars and cents intelligently with your future employer—and, just as importantly, being able to talk openly about your financial affairs with your future spouse. The inability to handle and discuss money has destroyed many marriages.

Whatever Vocation You Choose In Life, You Will Always Be Held Accountable for the Numbers!

I don't care what your major is or what career you choose. Your success in life will always be about the numbers. Whether you are in business to create profits or you are in a nonprofit organization, no matter your job title or job description, you will always be held accountable for the financial health of the organization. Don't be foolish to think, "I am a creative type and I just don't understand numbers!" Money is one area you don't want to take lightly. Discipline yourself to manage your money. Money is also one area that you don't put off trying to figure out until you have time. Make time now. Don't ever go to bed without taking care of your financial paperwork.

Performance Reviews: Get Used to Being Held Accountable
Many young people right out of college want responsibility but have a hard time being held accountable. You cannot have responsibility without accountability. Get comfortable in discussing your school performance, job performance, and finances with complete openness and honesty. Start by having complete detailed performance conversations with your parents! Your performance and money management will be something you will have to discuss the rest of your life with your boss, clients, investors, bankers, creditors, insurance agents, and your spouse.

Take a College Accounting Course!
The best advice when it comes to learning about the numbers and knowing how to read a financial statement is take a beginning accounting course in college. Your career may have nothing to do with accounting, but every position in management or leadership requires you to be responsible for the numbers. You may hate math. You may hate numbers. But whatever you have to do to force yourself to get through an accounting course, DO IT!!! You will never regret having this background in numbers. Reading and managing a profit and loss statement is an important life skill you will actively make use of the rest of your career. Being a good money manager is critical to your career success and harmony in your family life.

Famous Dave's Key Lesson: Wealth does not come from what you earn! Wealth comes from the size of your investment portfolio. Your goal should to be fully financially literate as much as possible. and I don't care if your goal in life is only to be a ceramic pottery maker! You need to take care of your money.

A BIG IMPORTANT LESSON: Don't lend people your money!
AN EVEN BIGGER LESSON: Don't borrow money from your friends!

The quickest way to turn a friend into an enemy...
lend him money.
~Wisdom of the Universe

Learn the Wonders of Compound Interest

Your investment portfolio gets created when you can save money consistently day after day, week after week, month after month, and year after year. Then invest your savings where your investment can grow through compounded interest. Wealth does not happen overnight, so DON'T EVER listen to anyone telling you there's a way to get rich quick! If they do...*seriously, run from them*!!!

Buy Your First HOME ASAP

One of the best things you can do right after high school or college is to start saving for a down payment to buy your first home. I know students who earned money all through high school and then bought a house when they went to college. They rented out the other rooms to pay for their own housing and the mortgage. When they graduated, they sold the house and made additional money from the sale of the house! Not only did this give them a bigger down payment for their next home, it gave them a great head start building their credit history.

> *I don't know what the 7 Wonders of the World are, but I do know that the 8th Wonder of the World is compound interest!*
>
> ~Baron von Rothschild
> Influential 18th-Century Banker (also attributed to Benjamin Franklin, Bernard Baruch, and Albert Einstein)

Don't Be Embarrassed to Say NO If You Can't Afford Something

There will be times when your friends will want to drag you along to something and it is not in your budget. It's perfectly OK to say, "I really can't afford it right now." Your friends will not judge you and they will understand. Don't get yourself all out of whack trying to keep up with students who have unlimited budgets or all the latest stuff. Be happy with what you've got. Don't ever let your pride make you the "big shot," foolishly spending money you don't have.

SUCCESS SKILLS 101: Make Financial Literacy A Priority! Start By Reading: *Rich Dad Poor Dad* **by Robert Kiyosaki.**

This is a great book to help you get started understanding how to build a financial portfolio and take charge of your financial affairs. I love this book so much that I give it out to all my associates and many of them have told me that they wished they had read this book 20 years ago! So you have a head start reading this book now. Also in the back of the book *Rich Dad, Poor Dad* is a great game to learn financial literacy. The game is called Cash Flow 101. It is the best game to learn how to navigate the unfamiliar waters of the financial world of investing. If there ever was a subject area in which you would want mentoring, this would be it. Find someone successful you know and trust and ask for their advice. Most importantly, you are responsible for the financial decisions you make in life, so a strong word of advice: Know where your money is at all times. Know how to budget. Know how to save. Know how to safely invest your money. Never, never, never put all your trust in someone who is investing your money—check everything out, and recheck! Don't take anyone's word for anything that has to do with your money. A word to the wise: When it comes to money, it isn't about trust, it is about financial responsibility. You will be held accountable, so go ahead and ask the tough questions!

If Savings is the mother of wealth, then Time is the Father, and Great Fortune is the child!

~Famous Dave Anderson
Founder of the World's Greatest BBQ Joint!

CHAPTER TWENTY

Great Ideas to Help You Get the Most Out of Your College Investment

The following is a series of great ideas and strategies to help you get the most out of your four years in college. Study them, embrace them, and you'll have the best four years of your life!

Get Your Priorities Straight Right From the Get-Go

Many students have sabotaged their college experience by trying to be someone else or they spend their energy trying to impress people with stuff that doesn't really matter. Get your priorities straight right from day one. There will always be people who have the latest stuff and that is just the way life goes. Sure, it's fun to have the latest stuff, but is that what's really important? We all want to be accepted and sometimes we feel less of a person because we're not accepted into the most popular clique, but is that really what's important in the greater scheme of life? Remember, it's not always cool to be cool! It's more important for you to be you. Be happy with you. Be true to yourself and you'll find the right people will gravitate towards you.

> *Isn't it odd... the people we're most often trying to impress are the people who have no idea we even exist? What's even goofier is that the most embarrassing dumb things I've ever said were made while I was trying to impress people who could care less...*
>
> ~Famous Dave Anderson
> Founder of the World's Greatest BBQ Joint!

Will Your Friends Help You Achieve Your Greatest Dreams?

This is a very important question you must answer with complete and brutal honesty: "Will the people you are hanging with help you achieve your life's greatest goals?" Here's another question to ask yourself: "How do these people react when faced with adversities? Are they blameful? Do they whine, complain, and make excuses?" If so, then you are hanging around the wrong people. Winners and successful people, when faced with problems, don't make excuses or act blamefully. Instead, they get charged up and get busy on finding positive solutions. They believe there is always an answer!

You Become the Average of the People You Hang With!

Remember this sage advice: You become like the people with whom you associate. If you hang with slobs, you will be a slob. If you hang with partiers, you will be a partier. If you hang with people who are striving to make their dreams come true and are challenging themselves to be better, there's a good chance you will achieve all your dreams, too. Look around you. Do your friends look like they can help you achieve your greatest dreams? Will the goals of your friends help make the world a better place?

Make sure the people you hang around with will challenge you to higher goals. Your dreams are so important you can never let other people hold you back from accomplishing your special plans for your life. Don't let the impulsive behavior of your peers veer you off track from your goals. The friends who will challenge you to greater accomplishments will be the friends you remember the most in college. Cultivate a network of lifelong, inspiring, challenging friends.

> *Your language will be that of your friends. Your reputation will be that of your associations. Your success will reflect the quality of the people who trust you. Look around you... what does that tell you?*
>
> ~ James W. Anderson
> Entrepreneur, Author, Speaker

Learn the Value of Non-Attachment

One of the hardest lessons you will learn in life about the people you associate with is... you will become just like them. Is this good for you? If not, practice *non-attachment*. There are times when you have to make some hard decisions to separate yourself from your old friends. Often, it is your friends, neighbors, and well-meaning relatives that hold you back in life. Surround yourself with only positive people who are working diligently to make their own goals a reality and whose goals are congruent with your goals.

Be Nice, Respectful, and Cheerful to All People

Throughout life you will find that certain groups of people tend to gravitate towards each other. Sometimes these cliques can ignore others who don't fit in with their way of thinking or interests. Whether you find yourself in one of these groups or you are on the outside, the most important thing is for you to *be nice* to all people. Remember, we all have our own odd quirkiness! Yes, Even you!!!

> *Look at everything as though you were seeing it either for the first or last time. Then your time on earth will be filled with glory!*
>
> ~Betty Smith
> Award-Winning American Author

Yes, Unfortunately, There Are People Who Don't Like You!

One of the toughest lessons I had to learn the hard way was there are people in the world that are just not going to like you. There is nothing you can do about it, so don't let it bother you. It's just life. Usually the toughest challenges that twist a knife in your gut are caused by breakdowns in relationships. These challenges are given to you by the Universe to test your spirit, your courage, and your perseverance to never give up. When you don't give up, the Universe rewards you with opportunity! Organizations look for people who don't melt under pressure.

Don't Ever Be Judgmental

Be accepting and welcoming to all. Everyone matters. Important advice: Get out of your comfort zone and try to meet people outside of your group. Always be expanding your horizons.

Here's a key thought: Your ability to connect socially with all types of people will be very critical to your career success. You never know when the person you befriend might be your future boss or your biggest client!

> *Be nice to the nerds, they may help you fix your computer...but more importantly, you are probably being nice to your future boss!*
>
> ~Famous Dave Anderson
> Founder of the World's Greatest BBQ Joint!

Diversity On the College Campus

This is a subject that needs to be better understood by all students and this subject particularly hits home for me. I am a Native American; my dad is a Choctaw Indian from Idabel, Oklahoma, and my mom is from the Lac Courte Oreilles Ojibwe tribe in Hayward, Wisconsin. Throughout my school years, I always felt like somewhat of an outsider. Many times, I just wished someone would have said "Hi!" to me. While schools today are cognizant of diversity and encourage diversity, we still have a long ways to go. Go out of your way and say "Hi!" to someone who looks like they need cheering up!

Diversity and Racial Discrimination Are Real Issues

You may be someone who just doesn't think about racial discrimination, but "just not thinking about it" and being ignorant of the different races, different sexual orientations, difference in religious views, political views, and poor vs. the wealthy is not a good approach for your college experience or your real-world career experience. Today, diversity is not only mandated by law, it is the reality of a changing world environment that requires everyone to be somewhat knowledgeable or respectful of the diversity of other people. Don't fall into this trap of ignorance. Let's appreciate and celebrate all people!

Become the Role Model of "Team Spirit" for Your School

Begin right away to become your school's biggest, raving, loyal fan. Attend orientation activities. As hokey as it may seem, go ahead and get involved—it's all about cultivating team spirit. Know the history of your school. Wear your school colors. Get to know the history of the town you will call home for the next four years. Being the role model for team spirit will also help get you noticed in your real-world job. Employers value employees who are big flag wavers for the company.

Don't Be Like Two Ships Passing In the Night!

Yes, it's uncomfortable walking into a strange room filled with strangers—but go ahead and shake off the jitters, smile, and introduce yourself. Say "Hi!" to all people. If you think you are uncomfortable, just remember the other person feels just as uncomfortable. Meeting strangers and connecting will be a critical career skill you can develop now in college. Don't be too cool and think some school activity is beneath you. Success is built on relationships and getting involved in your school activities.

Don't underestimate the value of getting involved, as your extracurricular activities will be gold on your resume. "Getting involved" is different than just "hanging out," and hanging out doesn't cut it on a resume! However, be careful: You will be bombarded to join everything. You don't want to spread yourself too thin. Make sure you find the right campus activity that will help you grow and achieve your academic and career goals.

Teamwork is the ability to work together toward a common vision. The ability to direct individual accomplishments toward organizational objectives. It is the fuel that allows common people to attain uncommon results.

~Andrew Carnegie
An American Industrialist and Major Philanthropist

Increase Your Expertise and Knowledge by Tutoring

Mentoring or tutoring will be great resume-building stuff. *Helping others succeed is one of the great essential character strengths of a great hire!* Employers delight in seeing this type of participation on a resume. It's also a known fact that the best way to strengthen your course mastery is to tutor and teach someone else.

> *Better than a thousand days of diligent study is one day with a great teacher.*
>
> ~Japanese Wisdom

SUCCESS SKILLS 101: Knowing How to Teach Is a Gift!
At one time, hoarding knowledge was thought to be job security. Today, the skill of helping others succeed is a valuable career skill. Learn how to teach. Learn how to share knowledge. What you learn from this book, share with your fellow classmates. Your teaching skills to help others succeed will make you highly valuable to the marketplace!

Student Groups Will Strengthen Your College Experience

Any fears of unfamiliar social settings will be overcome by your getting involved in different student groups on campus. The benefits are huge, not only because it makes your college experience a great one, but it's especially beneficial for your ability to navigate social settings in your career. Being active in a club is a great opportunity to learn leadership in groups, planning, organizing, and practicing your social skills. Being part of a student group will help strengthen your college experience, and it's great to be part of something that may provide long-term networking connections. Don't miss out on this opportunity. Your involvement will create fond memories and close friendships that will last a lifetime!

> *My whole purpose in life is just to make you happy!*
>
> ~Famous Dave Anderson
> Founder of the World's Greatest BBQ Joint!

Refer to Your Resume to Decide Which Student Groups You Should Get Involved With

Find a group that best represents the goals you have set out for yourself and best suits your interests: band, school sports, intramural sports, ROTC, fraternities, sororities, religious, political, ethnic, nationality, career groups (like architects, engineers, business, law, journalism, theater), and debate... just to name a few.

> *Get involved in something larger than yourself. It will take you out of your comfort zone, but it's here that you will find your meaning for life's higher purpose.*
>
> ~Famous Dave Anderson
> Founder of the World's Greatest BBQ Joint!

Strategies for Getting Your Pick of Professors, the Best Class, the Best Class Time Slot

Get to Know Your Professors and Make Sure They Know You!

The best grades I received were from professors I was able to establish a relationship with in college. One of the helpful "head's up" tips I received from a good friend, Dr. Rick St. Germaine: When you introduce yourself, make sure you fully introduce yourself and give your professor a warm handshake. Rick said, as a professor, he found it helpful when a student first introduced himself or herself and gave a warm, welcoming handshake. A professor meets so many students, they can't always remember everyone, and a proper introduction helps get the conversation off to a great start.

Make Your Professors Stakeholders in Your Success.

All professors want their students to succeed and want to create relationships with students who are ambitious and striving to do well in their classes. Sharing how serious you are about learning gives the professor a stake hold in your success. Asking questions both in class and after class will make an impression on your professor. When you are on the edge for a grade, your impression will be the tipping point for a better grade.

Remember, professors are human too.
If you can pick up little things about who they are and what their interests are, you can have something to talk about when you visit them. Holiday cards, thank you notes, and sending them interesting articles in their field of research are always appreciated by your professors. Mastering the skill of "I was thinking of you" is creating the foundation for developing powerful networking skills.

Your Relationship With Faculty Will Mirror Your Real-World Relationship With Your Future Boss
Here's the Key Lesson: The kind of relationship you establish with your professors and other faculty will most likely be the same relationship you will have with your future boss or supervisor in the real-world. Learn how to establish nurturing relationships with people in authority. If you can't establish a great working relationship with your professors, then most likely you will have a tough time establishing a relationship with your future employer. Get out of your comfort zone and go meet your professors!

Make Good Use of Your Professors' Office Hours
Students rarely utilize their professors during their office hours. Don't pass up this free resource; it's like getting free tutoring from the master! More importantly, professors are top thought leaders in their industry and often have critical connections to key industry employers or community organizations. Professors are often well connected to the movers and shakers in your field of interest. They can help you find internships, help craft resumes that best reflect your strengths, and write glowing letters of recommendation for you!

Take College-Level AP Courses in High School to Get Your Pick of the Best Classes, the Best Class Times, and the Best Professors
If you want a head start in college, hopefully you are reading this book while you are still in high school. Challenge yourself to take college-level Advanced Placement courses in high school.

Here's how class selection is parceled out: seniors and athletes get first pick of professors, the best classes, and the best time slots. Next, the hierarchy goes down the line: juniors, sophomores, and then incoming freshmen. Here's a great strategy for beating all other freshmen: In high school, as early as you can, start taking college-level AP courses. The more college courses you can take in high school will give you the ability to supersede all other freshman for the first pick of courses and professors. This is an excellent example of how a Slight Edge Difference will separate you from the masses!

THIS IS HUGE!!!... Volunteer to Be a TA

Famous Dave's Key Lesson: Your success in creating a relationship with your professors will help you stack the deck for getting A's in your classes by volunteering to be a TA, or Teaching Assistant. Professors have heavy workloads and depend on TAs to help them prepare for class, carry their books from their office to class, help them make copies, and help them research. *If you are organized, dependable, and have a good work ethic, you might qualify to be a TA.*

What's great about this is, if you are very helpful to a professor, you will be developing a great relationship with this professor and they will become a raving, loyal ambassador for you around campus! They will enthusiastically brag about you to other professors. When the word gets around, you will have top-of-mind awareness within the faculty and administration. This will help you immensely with your grades. More importantly, your professors will help you get into the classes you want and write letters of recommendation for you for financial aid or letters of recommendation for getting a job.

How to Let Your Professor Know You Would Like to Help Them

The best way to get selected for being a TA is to make an appointment with your professor at the beginning of the term. Make sure you do your research on the professor. See if they update their syllabus every year.

Check to see if this professor has written any books; there is a good chance they are writing another book or and they may need help in their research. Once you have made your appointment, here's what you say: *"I noticed you update your syllabus every year and I am in the library all the time. I wanted to see if I could help you find books for your research, do your copying, or help you as a TA? I would love to help you and hopefully you will help share your insights with me so I can get the most out of your classes?"* You will find only 30 percent of the professors may be real jerks and will blow you off. Don't let that discourage you—just remember 70 percent of the professors love to teach and really value their TAs. Just keep asking until you find a professor that will be extremely grateful for the free help. An insider tells me that when a professor finds a TA that really helps them, they will sing their praises to the whole world!

> *The dream begins with a teacher who believes in you, who tugs and pushes and leads you to the next plateau, sometimes poking you with a sharp stick called truth.*
>
> ~Dan Rather
> America's Leading News Anchor

Picking the Right Professor

In sports, the team owners spend a great deal of time, energy, and dollars to recruit the best talent. In life, companies spend an equal amount of time, energy, and dollars to recruit top talent. As a college student you are a customer of the college and you have a right to choose the best courses, best professors, and best time slots available. Find professors who have real-world experience and not just book knowledge.

Check Out www.RateMyProfessor.com

One good way to check out your professors is to go to RateMyProfessor.com and check out every professor that teaches the class you need to take or would like to take. Students will tell you how the professor grades, what kind of tests, essays, and specific homework that may be required. They will pretty much tell you how to get the best grades possible. There is one caveat: Not all reviews will be flattering to the professor, and you should disregard all the worst reviews, as these generally are submitted by angry students who got whacked on their grades. Read enough where you get a good feel for the professor and what you might learn from taking their course.

Department Professor Evaluations
You can also get professor evaluations from the department. These are public records. Feel free to ask for them.

Don't Always Take the Easiest Courses!
Don't be scared if the class is deemed hard by student reviews. If your life's dream is to be excellent in a certain profession and this professor has been reviewed as hard but good, this professor would be a good choice for you. However, if this course is a required course that you must take but the course it not particularly relevant to your life's passion, then you may want to find an easier professor.

When a Professor Is Tough On You
Some friendly advice: Sometimes your professors may seem really hard on you. It's probably needed. Many times we get caught up into our comfort zone and we need to be jerked out of it so we can learn. Embrace being challenged. Some of the best employers to work for may also be the most challenging bosses. So if you think your college professor is hard on you, wait until you get a real job when your boss has to make deadlines, increase productivity, and increase profits. In college, you can drop a tough course with a challenging professor. In the real world, if you don't perform, your boss will drop you like a hot rock. Best advice: Get used to being challenged. Don't think it's personal or think you are being picked on; see it as your opportunity to get better. Being challenged by your mentors will bring out your best!

Take Your Hardest Classes In the Summer
You may want to consider taking your hardest classes during the summer, when you focus all your energies on one or two classes. It is also believed that professors tend to be more accessible for you to get after-class help.

Challenge Yourself, But Be Careful: Don't Overload Yourself

College is designed to help you master self-discipline and stretch you to find out what you are really capable of achieving. BUT don't try and overload yourself until you have mastered your study habits. While it's important to participate in a few campus activities, don't become a student who is always rushing off to another class or activity and is usually late for everything.

> *Consult not your fears but your hopes and your dreams. Think not about your frustrations, but about your unfilled potential. Concern yourself not with what you have tried and failed in, but with what it is still possible for you to do.*
> ~Pope John XXIII

Don't Schedule Back-to-Back Classes or Activities

When it comes to classes that may be difficult for you, try not to schedule back-to-back classes, or classes followed immediately by a campus activity. You need time before and after class to regroup, go over your notes about information you might be struggling with; and you need to make note of how you are going to resolve the things you don't understand. Rushing from one class to another without a break to regroup is not highly recommended .

Your Bio-Clock and Performing at Peak Levels

We all have natural times of peak mental alertness and peak energy. Just like we have natural times where we power down. You have up to three hours of 100 percent peak performance and about the same amount of time when you are completely zapped. Pay attention to your bio-clock, and during your most productive times you should be taking your hardest classes.

Power Study During Your Peak Bio Times

When you are at your biological peak times, when you are fully mentally alert, this is when you want to do your best studying for your hardest courses. For example, you may get more out of one hour or two hours of study during your peak times than if you studied for five hours during the time when you were all zapped of your mental and physical energy. Your toughest classes should be best strategized to fit your internal bio-clock when you are at peak performance. This is also a key strategy for studying for important exams. Study for your hardest course exams when you are the most alert. Just knowing this bio-clock strategy could increase your grade level by one whole grade!

Eat Your Elephant

Success is like eating an elephant. You eat it one bite at a time. You don't look at the whole elephant and think it's impossible! Succeeding in college is the same. You don't look at the whole semester and start thinking how tough it's going to be. Here's one major key to your success in college: Look at each every class like it was its own individual project. Don't get inundated by looking at how tough the whole semester might be. Take your calendar and write down all your assignment due dates, test dates, and study times. Follow your plan without fail. Set yourself up for success by focusing on only one day at a time.

Learning In Chunks Consistently Over Time Is Best

Don't try and cram everything all at once. Study every day without fail. When you try to cram, you actually jam yourself up. Stuffing your head is like a picture on an Etch A Sketch: You get all your learning wires haywire. Your brain cells do a much better job absorbing stuff over a period of time that is constantly fed to your brain in chunks.

Success is the sum of small efforts,
repeated day in and day out.
~Robert Collier
American Self-Help Author

CRITICAL: Don't Move On Until You Have a Game Plan for Learning Something You Don't Understand!

As you study, you keep layering on information and your brain works to remember and process this information. If you don't understand something, get help immediately. Your professors are teaching you in a way in which everything you learn is building on a foundation. Don't set yourself up for failure by passing by something without having a strategy for knowing how you are going to learn the stuff you are having problems with. It will haunt you later. Last-minute studying for a test should only be reviewing of information that you should already know. Don't fool yourself that you are going to learn everything the night before a big test.

YOU HEARD IT HERE FIRST...
REVEALED: The Real Secret to Test Taking!!!

There are a lot of good ideas floating around on the Internet about how to ace your exams and tests, including whatever good advice your own school will provide you. But I have never seen this test strategy discussed anywhere before, so this is one of my profound gems! If you are studying for a test, do not eat pizzas, cheeseburgers, or any fast food before a test! This stuff is greasy and grease will sludge up your blood. Blood is rocket fuel for the brain. The brain is the largest organ that uses the greatest amount of blood for oxygen, which is a good reason to exercise. You will study better and feel more alert and have better recall if you cut out grease and carbs. Go veggie and exercise routinely several days before a test. Avoid salt, as it will constrict your blood vessels. Drink lots of water so you are fully hydrated. Not staying fully hydrated will also sludge up your blood.

Avoid sugar and carbohydrates, so you don't have highs and lows and crashes while taking a test. Take plenty of B vitamins, which will help control your nerves and avoid caffeine. When your school tells you not to stay up all night cramming, there is a lot of wisdom to this advice. Your mind works better refreshed, and you have better recall. Get your rest!

SUCCESS SKILLS 101: Your Health and Nutrition
This is one area that you need to learn on your own, as most doctors will never sit you down and discuss a nutrition plan for your life. College is the Super Bowl, the World Series, a championship fight. It is so important that you succeed because your success in excelling at A-grade-level college work sets you up for life. So, if professional athletes will hire the best nutrition specialists to guide them to perform at the very highest level of performance, your college performance should be no different. Top athletes, when getting ready for a playoff game or in Ultimate Fighting, will go veggie. They are in top condition to perform in the biggest game of their career. Your college exams should be no different. Studying is not enough. Your health, rest, and mental awareness all are critical to your success in school. Sure, it's great to party and have fun, but do this after your exams.

YouTube Videos: A Treasure Trove of "How-to" Information
YouTube University... I wish YouTube videos were around when I was struggling in school! Today, you can find online some of the best tutorials on just about anything. There are great YouTube videos on how to create concepts for your papers, how to write effectively, how to survive college, how to get the most out of college. Many successful professors have their "insider tips" online. Many helpful students have their own relevant tips on how to succeed and survive in college, and these videos are amazingly good! Such videos are usually about five minutes long, but pack some great tips, strategies, and advice that could help you immensely!

One machine can do the work of fifty ordinary men. No machine can do the work of one extraordinary man!
~Elbert Hubbard
American Writer, Artist, and Philosopher

Get To Know Your Academic and Career Advisors

Famous Dave's Key Lesson: I have seen many careers flounder because an employee has had a hard time discussing job issues with their boss. Probably one of least-used resources at college is your academic and career advisor. Cultivate your confidence now by establishing an open, honest relationship with your college advisors. Schedule regular updates with your advisor. They have seen it all and they have heard it all. You can confide in them about how your college life is going. When you ask for help, it is NOT an indication that you can't handle the rigors of college. Asking for help demonstrates your maturity and wisdom to ask for help. All students, brilliant or average, have needs that they have to discuss, and this is only normal.

Your advisors can help you plan better programs for your semester or help you decide which courses are better for your career plans. Asking for help is a good habit to get into, as your future employers will respect you for knowing when something is over your head and you are mature enough to get help. Many business blunders are caused by inexperienced employees who are too arrogant to ask for help, Don't let this be you!

Here's a hint I learned from a bright student who learned how to cultivate a great relationship with their advisor: If something goes wrong, say you are one credit short, the more your advisor knows you, the more they are likely to help you out and may possibly waive the credit! Consider your advisors as your support team. Treat your support team as you would your most trusted mentors, or like family. Remember them at holidays and send them cards or a thank-you!

He who is afraid of asking is ashamed of learning.
~Danish Proverb

SUCCESS SKILLS 101: Peak Performance and Accountability
In college, you will not have people telling you what to do. Immediately learn how to create accountability in your life. Get used to reporting in to your parents. Discuss your progress with your college advisors. All peak performers in life thrive on being held accountable—it's a way to measure up. Get used to explaining where you are in all areas: grades, dorm life, financial matters, and personal issues. You will never be given responsibility if you fight being held accountable. For the rest of your life, you will be held accountable and expected to discuss your performance. Get used to it now while you are in college.

Famous Dave's Key Lesson: Share your frustrations or failures in a positive way. Learn how to accept your mistakes, goof-ups, and downright unbelievable messes as great learning opportunities.

A Word to the Wise: Don't ever be blameful when discussing your transgressions—you will only look increasingly more guilty and like a weak, sniffling crybaby. Fess up immediately and make amends. Do the right thing! Best advice: "No surprises! EVER."

Join Your School's Mentorship Program
Once you have identified your career path, join your school's mentorship program. This is an incredible fast track to mentoring with an industry leader, which also could provide very meaningful job recommendations or internships for the job of your dreams! Make sure you ask about the school's mentorship program as soon as possible. Beside career mentors, you can also create a mastermind alliance—which could include your parents, religious leaders, coaches, your boss at work, and community leaders. Invite them to dinner and share your hopes and dreams with your alliance. You will find that, if you ask, most authority figures will be glad to spend a few moments with you and share their career insights and experiences.

> **Those who don't seek help...**
> **are ignorant to their true potential.**
> ~James W. Anderson
> Entrepreneur, Speaker, and Author

Learn a Foreign Language That You Can use!

Hopefully, you have taken a foreign language in high school and it's a language you can use. I took Latin in high school because it was the cool thing to do, and I have regretted it to this day because I have never been able to use it anywhere! I wished I had taken Spanish or French, languages that I could actually use if I traveled. Continue learning a foreign language in college. Many employers give higher credit to multi-language-speaking job applicants, especially in an ever-increasing global marketplace.

Travel the World

One of the best things I did in my last year of high school was to travel abroad for three weeks with my school. We stayed in student hostels and traveled by bus through 13 European countries. This is why I recommend you learn a language you can actually speak somewhere. Expand your horizons and discover our awesome world! While you are in college, jump at the opportunity to study overseas.

Every college graduate will tell you they missed the opportunity of a lifetime by not studying abroad, and regretted it. You will create friendships and fond memories that will last a lifetime. More importantly, you gain global relevancy to what life and the marketplace are like for other people living in different countries. Employers also like to see study abroad on a resume, as it signals that you are a world traveler and you have the responsibility and the maturity to navigate the nuances of international travel. Don't pass on this opportunity; it will be the highlight of your college experience!

> *Twenty years from now you will be more disappointed by the things you didn't do than by the ones you did do. So throw off the bowlines, sail away from the safe harbor. Catch the trade winds in your sail. Explore. Dream. Discover.*
>
> ~Mark Twain
> Legendary American Author and Humorist

Don't Let Your Backpack Become Your Filing System!

Learn how to set up a proper filing system in your biggest desk drawer. Can you imagine showing up for your first day on your dream job with your backpack? Proper filing skills are one organizing skill that will help you tremendously throughout your career. There is absolutely no reason for you to go to college if you don't learn how to set up a proper filing system! If you don't know how, ask and get help. Create a file folder for each class. Have an information sheet listing your professors' and your advisors' contact information, office hours, and any information about your classes or personal information about your professors like family, hobbies, favorite sports, etc. Provide information on tutors, work labs, peer review workshops, and pre-exam review sessions (don't miss these ever!). Discipline yourself to get things done ahead of schedule and you'll never get behind.

THE POWER OF JOURNALING: Don't Keep Your Million-Dollar Ideas On Scraps of Paper!

The difference between highly successful professionals and your average everyday manager is that the highly successful professional journals in a book and the average everyday manager writes things on Post-it Notes. Learn how to power journal. This is not about keeping a diary. Get a quality journal from any office supply store. You may be shocked to discover how much a book with nothing but empty pages can cost! But your journals are for a lifetime.

What You Write In Your Journals Is Priceless!

Journaling is a success strategy for detailing the important things that happen in your life, which could include important people you meet, powerful thoughts, and great ideas. Learn how to inventory your journal by placing tabs on important pages and then keeping an inventory list in front of the book.

If life is worth living, life is worth recording!
~Jim Rohn
America's Foremost Business Philosopher

Use Old-Fashioned Three-Ring Binders, NOT Spiral-Bound Notebooks

The common tendency in college is to use spiral-bound notebooks. Instead, keep a system of three-ring binders for each class. Keep one three-ring binder that you can use for all your daily classes and, once you are back at your dorm room, then you can place each class's notes in a three-ring binder that you keep for each class alone in your dorm room. You can keep your syllabus handy, place pocket inserts, and dividers for each class in your binder. You will be more efficient and you are developing organizing skills for life.

Helpful Memory Tricks You Need to Master

In college and throughout your career, there will be times when you will need to memorize key information. I am amazed at how executives struggle to memorize something when developing simple little memory joggers can make them look they have photographic memories. Create key topic groupings and assign a keyword, picture, or number to each concept. Cultivating this skill in college will help you in your career when you have to make presentations. Being able to give presentations without notes makes you more effective and memorable.

Make a word, number, or picture for each concept. For example: For a social studies class in high school, we had a test to write down all fifty states. I placed all states in order by the alphabet and assigned a number according to how many states began with that number...

A C D F G H I K L M N O P R S T U V W
4 3 1 1 1 1 4 2 1 8 8 3 1 1 2 2 1 2 4

Today, 45 years later, I still remember this 19-number combination! The trick is to work both the numbers and the alphabet together, understanding that there are only so many states for the alphabet letter and that for some letters there are no states...and then everything falls into place. It's easier than you think! But that's the whole idea: how to figure out ways to memorize concepts or important facts for tests.

Consciously Think About Exercising Your Mind at All Times

Memorizing phone numbers, doing crossword puzzles, and playing chess are all excellent ways to keep your brain functional. Your brain is like a muscle... the more you use it the more it becomes agile. Your mental goal throughout life should be *"learning agility."* If you don't mentally stimulate learning, your brain will become slow and will atrophy.

Famous Dave's "Insider Secret": *Make an impression by standing out with quick answers.* As an employer, when I am in a meeting, I notice the employees who are quick on their feet to figure things out and I remember this when it comes time to assign an important task. Keep your mind active and quick.

AMAZE YOUR PROFESSORS AND CLASSMATES: Learn How to Design and Use PowerPoint Presentations

In some classes, you may be required to give presentations. Just don't get up and read from your notes—learn how to use PowerPoint for your presentations. If your college has a class on PowerPoint presentations, make sure you take this class. This is one useful skill you will use in your career, and the more interesting you can make your presentations, the more successful you will be in influencing your clientele or making presentations to fellow employees. Learn how to create compelling handouts along with your PowerPoint presentation. Your handout should reinforce your presentation.

Student Leadership Jumpstarts Your Career

Consider running for an office within your group. College student groups are a great opportunity for you to test your leadership skills, and the skills you develop will jumpstart you in your professional career. People skills, "playing nice in the sandbox," being able to chair a meeting, getting your teammates to follow through on a project—these are probably the most important career skills you can ever learn, skills that will pay huge dividends throughout your life.

Real-World Job Skills Start NOW...Stand UP and Stand OUT

Discovering how *getting the job of your dreams begins Day One at college...* starts out with how you first appear to everyone <u>and</u> *how you first introduce yourself.* Be memorable! First impressions are important: You may be talking to your future boss, OR you may be talking to someone you may want to hire when you're the boss. All your contacts in college will be important throughout your life.

Never underestimate how crucial it is to improve your grooming, appearance, and your manners to be a professional even while you are in college. How you show up ready for success is remembered when it comes time for promotions and raises; it isn't always just about how you do your job. Your readiness for work, a positive attitude, and being well-groomed—helping the company succeed—are vital factors that are considered. These are skills you need to master now, while you are in college!

55% of All First Impressions Are Based on How You Show Up!

Here are some real interesting statistics on why it's so important not to treat your college experience casually. First, 55 percent of first impressions are based on appearance. How you are dressed, groomed and present yourself are critically important to your success. Next, 38 percent of the first impression is based on your non-verbal behaviors such as facial expressions, posture, or how your body language represents you. Only 7 percent of first impressions are based on what you have to say, according to a research study by the University of California, Los Angeles. But here's the thing: What you say may be vitally important, but if you show up looking like you just rolled out of bed, no one is going to want to listen to you no matter how important the things are that you have to say.

There are Three Types of People in The World
1. Those who make things happen.
2. Those who watch what happens.
3. And those who wonder what happened!

You Never Know Who You Will Meet On Campus

Dress up to go up! It's all about first impressions. Cultivate the habit of taking care of your appearance. Sure, it's OK to dress casual in college. But keep your appearance neat and clean—don't look like you just rolled out of bed. You never know who you will meet on a college campus, and first impressions count. Many company recruiters frequent college campuses. Many top company executives are on campus daily giving guest lectures on relevant topics. You may meet a friend's dad who happens to be the founder of a very successful company, and you may have an internship opportunity or a real job opportunity if you look like an up-and-coming student who stands out from the crowd. How you hold yourself, your body language, your cheerful smiles, and your positive spirit should be immediately noticeable.

You Can Never Earn Back Your First Impression

You never have a second chance to earn back your first impression. If you are on campus for any reason, make sure you look and act like you are ready to go to work. When you are in your dorm you can be as casual as you want. Here's some great advice from a shoeshine: You can't do deals in dirty heels! There is a lot of truth to this advice. Dress to impress. **Wise Advice From Walt Disney:** *"You are always on stage!"*

Your Social Skills, Manners, and Etiquette Need Practice

In a competitive job market, little things like your social skills may be the "slight edge" that gives you the defining difference between thousands of other job applicants. First impressions, your appearance, and social skills are more important in today's highly competitive marketplace. Employers size you up, trying to determine if you will present yourself as a successful representative of their growing company or organization. If you have that "magic glow," your prospective employers also know that you will attract other successful employees to their firm. Ask yourself, "Will my present attitude and behavior attract quality employees to join my company?"

Some "Inside Wisdom" From Me as a Business Owner: Make Your Company Glad They Hired You!

Here's how important it is for you always to be bright, cheerful, well-groomed, and glowing with optimism. As a business owner, I am forever meeting with new vendors, bankers, franchise owners, and new prospective employees. When I am giving a tour of my restaurants, I always know which employee is the brightest, best-groomed, and most cheerful that I want to introduce to my guests. I will purposely avoid introducing my guests to some employees, even though they are great employees, loyal, and do a good job—they just don't have that spark and they don't show well. Meeting an energetic, cheerful employee who bubbles with enthusiasm about working for Famous Dave's is priceless. It gives my guests the most favorable impression of our company and the best reasons why they should do business with us.

Revealed! The Secret Behind the Famous Dave Smile

People tell me that I have a great big smile. Here's my **Famous Dave's "Insider Secret!"** *I didn't always have a big smile and a big cheerful face!* Early on, I realized I needed to change how people perceived me. I would stand in my parent's basement for hours with a $5 mirror from Kmart and I would practice smiling, raising my eyebrow, and winking. Today, I can wink simultaneously with both eyes! I also worked on having big, round eyes when I smile. I purposely practice opening my eyes wide with one eyebrow raised when I smile, and today I consciously think about having to do this whenever I am having my picture taken. I share this stuff about me because we all have things we need to work on. Today, my smiley, cheerful face has graced the front cover of every newspaper and magazine in our industry and local communities. What do you have to work on?

> *Always remember to be happy, because you never know who's falling in love with your smile!*
> ~ Wisdom of the Universe

"Your Glow" Will Open Many Doors of Opportunity

Every day you are in college, get used to pumping yourself up so that you can be a spark of enthusiasm and positivity wherever you go. By the time you are ready for the workforce, you will have this glow about you that will make you irresistible to the marketplace. *Word to the wise:* Exercising every day will give you a natural glow about you, give yourself every opportunity you can create, so get into the habit exercising daily! Your energy level, a cheerful smile, and a well-groomed appearance will open many doors of opportunity long before anyone ever finds out you are a recent college graduate!

Make Employers Want to Hire You Right Now!

Work hard to create a positive image of yourself. Never dress for the job you're in now, always dress for the job you would like to have! Even if you are in college, you need to let the world know that you are ready. Don't let a prospective employer try and figure out what you will look like once you clean yourself up. Leave everyone with the impression that will make them think, "I can't wait for this student to graduate because I would hire them right now!"

The Best Way to Be Different and Stand Out From the Masses

If your desire is just to be different, the best way to be different and stand out from the masses is: 1) to be the hardest worker possible; 2) strive to be excellent at whatever you do; and 3) use your talents and skills to be "obsessively devoted to making others happy." I'll guarantee if you just do these three things, you will stand head and shoulders above anyone else!

> *Do not quit! Hundreds of times I have watched people throw in the towel at the one-yard line while someone else comes along and makes a fortune by just going that extra yard!*
>
> ~Joseph Cossman
> Creator of Drive-In Banks

Be Someone Your Classmates Want to Have On Their Team
Employers want to know how well you are going to get along with your fellow employees. They will also be trying to figure out how you will represent the company at important business meetings and social functions. Above all, employers are assessing your ability to meet key executives of the company's clients and your ability to entertain these clients. This reason alone is critical to why you need to think of your college experience as your on-the-job training. If you are uncomfortable now in meeting new people, you will have a tough time in your career. Get your fears out of the way now. Sharpen your social skills while in college. You need to be able to hit the ground running once you are hired.

Learn How To Successfully Navigate In A Social Setting Without Embarrassing Yourself
Fortunately, today we live in a world where you can get a jumpstart learning etiquette online. Start here—but when you can, I would highly recommend that you find a two-hour course on business etiquette so you can practice your skills with other real people. Learn how to properly shake hands, introduce others at a gathering, how to pass the salt and pepper shakers, which fork or spoon to use, and which water glass is yours—all are critically important to your on-the-job success.

Here's one extra good reason why you need some mastery of proper social skills: It would be terrific if you didn't embarrass yourself in front of the potential love of your life or this person's parents!

> *Buy something silly and wear it. A Groucho Marx nose with mustache, and glasses are my favorite. When the stress seems unbearable, when you've really reach the limits of your endurance, go into a bathroom, look into the mirror, put on your glasses, and ask yourself, "How serious is this?"*
>
> ~Loretta LaRoche
> Author, Humorist, Inspiring Speaker

SUCCESS SKILLS 101: Grooming and Social Skills Development
Just because you are in college doesn't mean you know how to dress and attend to your appearance. Your appearance and social skills are just as important disciplines to be studied with the same intense focus as your college courses. Don't trust your own ideas. I have seen college graduates in professional settings with the appropriate suit but their shirts are not ironed or the wrong color, their choice of ties is questionable, shoes unpolished, and their hair a mess. I have seen young women with great technical skills, but their makeup and choice of dress is sometimes unbelievable.

With the same reasoning you used to recognized how important it was to invest in a college education, invest in professional advisors to help you with a professional look and professional social skills. Search for "Executive Image Consultants" and "Business Etiquette." This investment into your "look" and "social skills" will be one of the best investments you can do for your Personal Brand and your career. In fact, it almost needs to be part of your college budget and planned for. If you can't afford a professional consultant, go online and search out free advice in these areas. Just don't disregard how important these critical career skills are to your future success.

Here's some great professional wardrobe advice for both men and women:

Go online and search...
Professional Dress Code Tips
By Donald K. Burleson

Clothes and manners do not make the man; but when he is made, they greatly improve his appearance.
~Henry Ward Beecher
Great American Preacher and Author

SUCCESS SKILLS 101: Organization, Cleanliness, and Neatness
Just because you are now free and independent doesn't mean you can live like a unorganized bum. How you take care of your desk, room, and class work will determine how you keep your office at work. Cultivating the skill sets in college to organize, file, and find information quickly will be another life skill that will serve you successfully in your career.

Word to the Wise: You can quickly tell who will succeed in life by how they keep their dorm room! What would your future employer find if they looked in on your dorm room.

Famous Dave's "Insider Secret": *Employers will always discover your dirty little secrets!* I know a very successful business owner in the hospitality business, who has his key staff inspect the car of the person they are considering hiring while they are in the interview. If the report comes back that the car is a mess, the person doesn't get hired! If the car is banged up, the person might have a drinking problem. There is a lot you can tell about a person's car, including cigarette butts in the ashtray. If a person can't take care of something as valuable as their own personal car, how are they going to respect your company's assets? Keep yourself organized, neat, and clean. You never know who is checking up on you!!!

Something to smile about...

> ***If a cluttered desk is the sign of a cluttered mind, what is the significance of a clean desk?***
>
> ~Dr. Laurence J. Peter
> American Educator and Author of *The Peter Principle*

Here's an Amazing "Success Studying Strategy": Invest In Two Computer Monitors!

At home I have the biggest and best computer, but I also have two huge computer monitors—and it is the best thing I have ever done to become more effective in my research and writing. You can keep all your research, access files, search the Internet, all while you have the your main document on your main screen. You will increase your productivity and your effectiveness by at least 50 percent because you are able to access key information quickly and have a series of research ideas front and center on another screen that helps you form ideas, concept, and thought strategies. You are able to zip documents around without having to constantly open and close files. Just the ability to cut and paste saves incredible time. Even while writing this book, I probably have 20 files open on my screens right now! Get two computer monitors: It will be the best thing you could ever do to help you succeed in your coursework and college. It's worth the investment!

> *The unfortunate truth about how fast technology is accelerating is technology can now produce information faster than man can engage good old-fashioned common sense or the wisdom to know better!*
> ~Famous Dave Anderson
> Founder of the World's Greatest BBQ Joint!

"iPod University" and Your "University On Wheels"

Get yourself a digital recorder or a mini-mike for your computer and ask your professors if you could record their lectures. Almost all will let you. Download them to your computer and burn a CD that you can play in your car, or download the lectures to your iPod. Listen to your lectures while you are driving around and while you are walking around campus. This will give you an unbelievable recall for tests, and hearing the lecture a second time around will give you better understanding; but you will also be able to identify key points that maybe you need to ask a question about at your next class or on a visit to the professor's office.

SUCCESS LIBRARY: Download Positive, Uplifting Audio Books

Start building your own personal Success Library of positive, inspiring audio books that you can buy at any major bookstore or online. Listen to positive, uplifting audio books that will keep you optimistic and positive when times get challenging. This is a great way for keeping your spirits up throughout your day. I have a few recommendations that are listed in the back of this book.

A Word of Advice, Seriously!

TURN OFF YOUR CELL PHONE ALL DAY! Make a decision that you will only use you cell phone during designated times. Don't even think of texting while in a classroom. The professors know exactly what you are doing and it is very disrespectful and could be the difference between grade points. Do not underestimate the memory powers of your professors. If they remember you texting in their classroom, it could be the deciding factor in a grade, or in their willingness to provide you with a job recommendation.

Being "Connected" Can Be Overwhelming Today

Today, we live in a generation where everyone is connected and you are almost addicted to your Facebook, Twitter, LinkedIn, emails, texting, etc., etc., etc. Set up a specific time that you will catch up; but stick to a time limit, otherwise your "staying connected" will eat into your study time. Set parameters for yourself and make sure you let your friends know your guidelines. You don't have to be embarrassed about setting up guidelines for how well you are connected. One day, you might look up from your smart phone and realize your life has just passed you by!

Word to the Wise: One of the rudest things I see today is an executive emailing or texting while in a meeting. Set yourself apart from these low-life executives by being the one listening intently to the speaker and furiously scribbling down notes.

Unless you've just discovered the cure for cancer,
you have no business texting in my classroom!
~Dr. Rick St. Germaine
Historian, Author, Professor, University of Wisconsin

Social Media and Getting Hired!

Unfortunately, it is very tough for colleges to keep their classes technology-relevant in today's rapidly accelerating, massive digital universe. But if you are going to be competitive, it's going to be up to you to know how to navigate digital media in your new job. If you are going to a college that has any classes on technology or social media marketing, I would advise you to take these classes.

Businesses today recognize how important it is to be technologically relevant to their customers or clients. Facebook, YouTube, Twitter, and LinkedIn are all now accepted forms of communication used by business and community organizations. Almost all employers will check you out on Google, Facebook, and LinkedIn before hiring. Make sure you have an updated LinkedIn page, as this is definitely will be checked out by recruiters and the human resources department.

Social Media Warnings!

As much as you are tempted, don't email, text, or put stuff on your Facebook, MySpace, Twitter, LinkedIn, or any other social media that could keep you from being hired. You may think you have removed stuff from your social media pages, but you need to completely understand this fact: Once you send something out into the digital universe, it is there FOREVER. You may remove it, but you never know if a friend, the school, the government, or somebody who doesn't like you has downloaded and saved it for eternity. Your digital record is FOREVER!

THIS IS SERIOUS! Don't get caught with stuff on your computer that you will be embarrassed explaining. If it shows up on your computer, you can be sure someone knows you downloaded it and you have a permanent record of downloading stuff you probably shouldn't be looking at, Again, your record of digital dalliance is FOREVER! So don't fool yourself believing that just because you have erased it from your computer, that is gone. The fact is, it is not. It is living on forever in the digital universe!

Employers Know All the Tricks to Find Stuff On You!

We live in a very litigious society today, and employers today are very cautious with who they hire. You can be sure they will do their due diligence. Employers today employ some of the best technology-security companies, who can find the very first text, digital download, emailed pictures you have sent or *emails that were sent to you*. What is in your digital history will be of concern to your employer, as they don't ever want to be part of a character lawsuit and have your past haunt the financial viability of their company. You may think you were having some innocent fun with your drunken party pictures, but an enemy of your employer will find your pictures and use it against your employer. Don't be blissfully ignorant of the dangers of what you post out into the digital universe.

You need to "be social" and not "do social."

~Jay Baer

Social Media Internet Guru

Yowza! Yowza! Yowza!
READ ALL ABOUT IT!

5 NEW STRATEGIES For Writing An Amazing Paper

There is plenty of great advice on how to write great papers available from your college or on the Internet. Make sure you find and put this advice to use. HOWEVER, here are some new strategies that may or not have been shared with you that could make all your papers stand out from the sea of sameness that is what everyone else hands in! One of these ideas might just give you the Slight Edge Difference!

1. **Discover How Reading the National Enquirer Can Make Your Papers Come Alive!** Have a killer headline that makes your paper memorable! Boring headlines can kill your paper the moment someone takes a look at it. Learn how to write compelling, evocative headlines that capture your reader's interest by studying tabloid headlines from the *National Enquirer, The Sun,* or *The Globe.* These tabloids are experts at writing compelling headlines that influence and create "calls to action." *(I heard this advice from James Malinchak, "America's College Success" speaker!)*

2. **Learn How to "Mind Map."** Also known as "concept mapping," this is one of the easiest ways to take your topic plus your research and create a methodology for creating a paper outline. There are some very easy-to-find details on concept mapping or mind mapping. Study these on YouTube. This one concept will help you immensely in all your subjects!

   - *Maximize the Power of Your Brain,* Tony Buzan Mind Mapping
   - *Mind Mapping* by Stephen Pierce
   - *Concept Mapping: How to Start Your Term Paper Research*

Concept mapping or mind mapping is a great help to understanding the structure of a subject. Concept mapping also helps create a visual understanding of the hierarchy of the relationship of individual points to the core of the subject. Concept mapping helps you think through ideas and solutions. Knowing how to create the hierarchy of how things work together will be helpful to you in your professional career.

3. **Focus On the Keywords.** Determine from your professor's assignment what the keywords are that are vital to writing this paper. Use these keywords in titles, subheads, and throughout the body of the copy. The use of keywords in writing your paper or thesis is a new twist in writing that begs to be understood in our new digital age.

    Famous Dave's "Inside Secret": *Today's digital world is ruled by "keywords."* The greatest strength you are learning here is your use and understanding of "keywords," not only in how they support your argument or research but how they connect you to the digital universe. This is a skill set you need to cultivate now! As the world becomes more digitally connected, *keywords are fuel for Internet search engines.* People will find you or your web pages through successful use of keywords.

4. **Use Online Job Clearinghouses.** Figure out how to use Elance, an online web source where you can find all kinds of freelancers. Find someone who will edit your paper for cheap. You may find someone who will edit a paper for just 20 bucks. (But don't hire them to write it for you. Your professor will know!) This book was edited by someone I found on Elance!

5. **Photo Enhancement.** If possible, use your own photos or free stock photos on the web, and add compelling captions that use keywords and help support the topics. Make sure you use the photos to enhance and support the paper, not just to fill up space.

CHAPTER TWENTY-ONE

Let's Party!
No Thanks
...I've Got to Go Study!

The Following Is Tough Stuff That Needs to Be Talked About
I need to share some personal tough stuff that I feel is important for you to be aware of in college. My goal is not to be preachy but to make you aware of the real problems that exist once you get settled into your career. I would be doing you a real disfavor if all I did was to share the good stuff and I didn't warn you about the most prevalent career-wrecking issues in the work place. Don't glance over this stuff thinking it doesn't pertain to you.

So, Here We Go... My Thoughts About Drinking and Partying
Many young people have done the most stupid things while drinking, and I was one of them. I thought I was just having fun; I didn't realize how quickly my life got out of control, and I had to leave college in my first semester. Long story short: 23 years later, when I was 42, my wife held an intervention on me and I went into treatment for alcoholism. Like most college students, I didn't start out to create a problem for myself. I was just having fun! You may be one of the fortunate ones that can have a few drinks and be OK, but there are many students that end up, over time, with a serious problem of alcohol or substance abuse.

Productivity losses attributed to alcohol and drug abuse were estimated at $246 Billion for 2009.
~National Institute on Drug Abuse

You May Not Have a Problem, But There Are Others In the Workforce with Drinking and Drug-Abuse Problems That Can Have an Impact On Your Career

As a bright-eyed student with all the aspirations to make it successfully in the real-world and anxious to enter the job force, you may not be one who drinks or will ever have a problem. You need to be fully aware of the consequences of drinking in the work place. I guarantee you, when you least expect it, someone who has a substance-abuse problem will affect your career.

Drinking and Drug Abuse Are Costly to Society

Drinking and drug abuse among U.S. workers can threaten public safety, impair job performance, and result in costly medical care, social dysfunctions, higher insurance costs, and other problems affecting employees and employers alike.

I have witnessed firsthand employees who can't control their drinking, and they do some really, really dumb, stupid things at company cocktail parties. If it were up to me, I would abolish company cocktail parties all together. However, having a cold beer and a drink is a social thing in today's society, and I am not making any judgments here. So, if you truly don't have a problem, great! Go ahead and enjoy yourself. However, just be aware of the long-term consequences if you start planning your day around your first opportunity to go out and get a drink.

It Is My Hope That My Being Open About My Own Drinking Problems Will Cause You to Be Aware That This Is a Very Real Issue In College and In the Workplace

Over the years, I should have been dead three times. Every student reading this book knows someone who has lost their life, directly or indirectly, because of drinking. Every student also knows a classmate that already has a drinking problem. They can't control themselves when they drink and they are in complete denial that they have a problem. You can talk to anyone in business and they can immediately tell you horror stories of friends and associates who have destroyed their careers because of drinking.

I Live a Grateful Sober Life Today

At the time of this writing, I have been sober for 15 years and I am living the best years of my life! Today, I am very open about my sobriety and feel my life's higher purpose is to share a message of hope. And it's OK to be honest about your drinking, especially if it something you feel you can't control. *There would be no Famous Dave's today if I had not sobered up.*

My Thoughts As an Employer Dealing With Addictions In the Workforce

Without a doubt, and I know many other employers will back me up on this: The number-one reason why employees are fired is because they have some form of substance-abuse problems. Usually, when we are having problems with an employee, we can trace the problems back to some form of drinking or drug addiction. If your ambition is to be in management, just be aware of alcoholism and drug abuse in the workforce—*and know that the first signs of alcohol and drug-abuse problems start showing up in college.*

College Drinking and Partying Can Cost You a Small Fortune!

No one sets out their first year in school to blow their budget on partying. But I have personally gone through this and I have seen many other students fall into the same trap. You're at school, your mom and dad aren't around, and you're free to do whatever you please. There's no question about it—anything and everything is available. What usually isn't available is common sense.

Most students are shocked to discover they've spent $4,000 partying over four years, or $1,000 a year, and it is not uncommon to find students who have spent $10,000 partying! I don't care how responsible you think you are; once you start partying, you lose willpower. Know your limits and show your maturity by sticking to the limits you have set for yourself. Once you're loose as a goose and you have no clue, all of a sudden, your whole week's budget gets spent in one night of crazy partying. A $1,000 expenditure sounds like a lot of money, but it's only two or three drinks several times a week, and it quickly adds up. $20 a week spent on drinks, times 50 weeks, is $1,000. So if you spend more than $20 two or three times a week on partying, now you can see why $10,000 spent over four years is not unfeasible.

Every student I have talked to says the same thing: They had no idea how much they spent on drinking and partying, and it is always a bigger number then they had thought. Money spent on drinking could have been a nice down payment on your first home or paying down your student loans! Drinking every week can very quickly add up to serious money over a year's time. Don't be ignorant about this!

DRUGS:
Don't Fool Yourself Into Thinking You Won't Be Found Out!

Word to the wise: If drugs show up, run from the room as fast as you can. Don't give into pressures when it comes to drugs. You will be surprised what is available and who is doing it. Getting a drug bust on your record will ruin everything you've worked for. Getting hooked on drugs is also something that will trip you up, as more and more employers are using the latest technology to test for drug use before hiring any key employee. Don't be ignorant and say it won't happen to you. DENIAL is actually the first sign you have a problem!

Employers Can Find Out Anything

Today, employers can find out anything; you can be sure your indiscretions will be found out. Many employers use sophisticated drug-detection procedures like testing your hair, and hair will keep your drug use and the types of drugs used forever until your hair either falls out or you shave your entire body! Employers have good reason to be concerned. Employers have invested thousands of dollars into every new hire, and even more if someone is hired for a management position. Employers want to make sure their investment is safe and not a waste of money by someone's extracurricular activities.

There Is No Shame In Asking for Help

If someone ever suggests to you that you need to think about your drinking, listen to them, as this is a warning that you may have a problem. They know your drinking is getting out of hand and you don't realize it.

Don't be ignorant and think they are the ones with the problem. Denial is a very tricky disease of the mind. If you have to say you don't have a problem, that is the first sign you have a problem. No one ever starts out believing that they are going to end up to be a drunk just by going out and partying with their friends. If you live your week thinking about how soon you can have a drink or get to a party, then drinking is starting to control your life. If all your social plans first revolve around going out for a drink, you have a problem.

Getting all "F_ _ ked Up!" Should Never Be Your Goal at Any Time!

Make Sure You're Brutally Honest With Yourself
HERE'S WHERE YOU NEED TO BE HONEST ABOUT THINGS: If anyone ever has to warn you about your drinking, even just one time, you may have a problem. Do something about it now, while you are young and it's easier to turn your life around. Denying you have a problem, especially when friends or loved ones talk to you about it, is ignorance and stupidity. Denial is weakness. There is no shame in asking for help. Please talk to someone and get help now, before it's too late. Listening to people who care for you, and then asking for help, demonstrates your maturity, strength, and wisdom.

Have Fun and Enjoy Your Partying
College is a time to have fun and a good time—but demonstrate your maturity by setting limits for yourself, and be responsible by sticking to your budget.

SEX...WOW!
This may be a book to get you ready for a successful career, so why am I talking about SEX? Because, over my years in business, I have witnessed firsthand the second most debilitating scourge besides alcoholism to a good company—and that is when employees and other employees, or supervisors and employees, lose their moral compass and they "hook up."

The fallout destroys the spirit in the office, and it destroys careers and families. Your sexual behavior in college will be a good indicator of how you will handle yourself in similar situations on the job. Remember: Your first goal is to get your diploma, not start a family. Protect your future. It's always about respect, and it's perfectly all right, and many times it is best just to say NO! Your commitment to your integrity and always doing the right thing will be your character's foundation and reputation once you get into the workforce.

You Are 100% Responsible for What Happens In Your Life!
College is a great opportunity for you to demonstrate your maturity as an adult. While there are many lessons to be learned in college, probably "being responsible" is one of the top ones. You can accomplish anything in life and make all your dreams come true if you take full responsibility for what happens in your life. Live your life free from excuses—because there are NO excuses in life.

Being Blameful Just Points the Finger Back to You
Never point a finger. Never be blameful. You can't blame your parents, you can't blame your education, you can't blame your teacher, you can't blame your race, looks, size, or anything else. The fact of life is and always will be: You are responsible for whatever happens in your life. Here's the deal: It's your decision, your choice. How you are going to deal with problem issues in your life depends on the choices YOU make.

Building a Great Reputation for Life
The underlying foundation of your college experience is for you to develop into your own person. Fundamental to that is the development of your reputation, your character, and your Personal Brand. The quality of your future spouse and the quality of your future employer will be a direct reflection of your character. Your reputation is to be protected like solid gold. Your reputation is for a lifetime. What kind of legacy are you leaving?

Don't Ever Give People a Reason Not to Trust You

Once you breach the trust of other people it is very difficult to earn back that trust. Integrity, honest, loyal, trustworthy, industrious, ethical, hard worker, team player, charitable, creative, brilliant, thoughtful, optimistic, passionate, enthusiastic: These are just some of the character traits that, hopefully, people will think of when your name comes up.

A great question to keep asking yourself: "How will I be remembered?" Another great question: "Can I explain this to the people I love?" These questions should be asked every time you are tempted to do things you know are not contributive to your life's greatest dreams.

A reputation once broken may possibly be repaired, but the world will always keep their eyes on the spot where the crack was.

~Joseph Hall
English Clergyman and Author

CHAPTER TWENTY-TWO

Final Thoughts

Congratulations for Making It Through Our Book This Far!
We sincerely hope the Success Skills 101 Strategies, Famous Dave's Key Lessons, and "Inside Secrets" have given you a real eye-opening look into what it takes to be successful in the real-world after college. It also has been our hope and prayer that you will discover how wonderfully gifted you are and how to use your giftedness to make the world a better place. We also hope you will have learned that life's struggles and adversities are not to discourage you but to challenge you to become a bigger and better person.

LIFE IS ABOUT CHANGE: Be Flexible, Creative, and Innovative
We are living in an unprecedented times of a rapidly accelerated, changing world where more change is happening in ONE day of the average college kid's life than in 10 years of the average adult's life! This is a huge statement. Students in college today are studying for jobs that may not even exist yet. Today, one new invention can wipe out an entire industry overnight. You have to be flexible and roll with the punches, or you will quickly become history. Throughout your life, you will be very disappointed to find things you hoped for will never be realized because the world has changed on you. You have to be creative, innovative, and flexible, as you will be challenged to find new ways to stay relevant. You will have to completely transform yourself many times throughout your career to stay competitive in a rapidly accelerated, changing global marketplace.

Graduating from college is not the end of your education. In fact, if you want to stay relevant and technologically updated, you are going to have to study harder than anything you've experienced in college. Because in college you were just studying for a grade; but in the real world, you will be studying just to keep your job and to stay one step ahead of a very competitive, raging marketplace.

Be a Possibility Thinker to Set Yourself Apart

Practice seeing opportunities and "what's possible" in every situation. This will set you apart from the masses. The easy thing is to point out all the reasons why something won't work. It's human nature to think you can't do some things. Your job is to continually feed your mind all the reinforcing beliefs that you are amazing and that all things ARE possible. Never set limitations on yourself. You are more amazing and capable than you think. Go ahead and do what you fear most. Give it a try and give it your best effort. Don't get discouraged if things don't always work out at first. Regroup and try again with even more determination. Be optimistic that you will succeed. Be a person that everyone trusts. Be a person who does what they say they will do. Be a person who stands up for the things they believe in. Be a person who stands up for people who need help. Be a person everyone can count on. Be a person of deep faith. You will amaze yourself about what you are really capable of achieving!

> *Whether you think you can or you think you can't, you're right.*
>
> ~Henry Ford
> Inventor of Mass Production and Founder of the Ford Motor Company

Famous Dave's Key Lesson: The difference between the *average* and *successful* is the average do just enough to get things right. The successful are relentless until they can't get it wrong.

Carpe Diem...Seize the Day!

Treat every day, school days, weekends, like gold. Every day matters. There are no practice days. You don't get to rehearse in the real world. Everything now counts. Wake up every single day with a positive, optimistic outlook that this day will be your best ever! Bring your "A" game. Play full out like every day was a championship game day. Don't ever put off until tomorrow what you can do today. You will never get this day back again. Be a positive influence in the world. Yesterday may have been a tough day, but good news: It's over! Start your day anew with renewed optimism and hope. Don't party to the point where you need a day to recover; you are wasting one of your precious days! You only have one life to live, so make the most out of it!

Today's A Brand New Day!

This is the beginning of a brand new day. God has given you this day to do with as you will. So pledge to yourself that this day shall be for gain not loss, good not evil, success not failure. For when tomorrow comes, this day will be gone forever, leaving in its place whatever you have traded for it.

~The Wisdom of the Universe

Smash Through All Your Self-Limiting Fears! Do Amazing Things That Scare the Heck Out of You!

While you are in college and while you have the physical agility and the mental alertness, do some fun things that will give you goose bumps. We all have fears and self-limiting thoughts or even self-defeating beliefs that hold us back in life. Make it your goal to do some fear-defying activities that will challenge you to stretch way outside of your comfort zone. I am a firm believer that the human mind, body, and spirit were meant to be challenged. Get outside your comfort zone to smash through all your self-limiting fears. Fear does not exist except within your mind. Banish fear from your mind forever!

Experience Life Full Out... Fuel Your Curiosity

Get a bunch of your friends and go whitewater rafting, skydiving, or Bungee jumping, do a challenging ropes course (make sure you zip-line!), go rock-climbing, compete in a marathon or a triathlon, fire walk, parasail, climb a mountain, go winter camping, tour Europe by train, walk the Appalachian Trail, walk the Great Wall of China, go hot-air ballooning, hike the Inca Trail, or see Machu Pichu. Make sure you have some wild, adventuresome stuff on your goals list!

Do something incredibly amazing that will give you great stuff to talk about the rest of your life. You will find the experience of doing fun, challenging, and interesting activities—activities that scare the heck out of you—will give you the self-esteem and the confidence to get out of your comfort zone at work. Make sure you write these down as goals, otherwise these incredible adventures will only be wishes. You will also be recognized as a team leader for encouraging your company team to join you as you continue to do spectacular things that test your spirit. More importantly, your family will say, "WOW!"

(I highly suggest if you attempt any of these activities, do so with a professionally trained supervisor and have checked with your doctor first.)

Follow Your Dreams and Make the World a Better Place

Finally, I want to leave you with the thought: If you focus all your God-given giftedness, attention, skills, and effort to making other people happy and the world a better place, you will surprisingly discover it will be the other people who will make your life richly rewarding beyond your wildest dreams!

My higher purpose in life is to make a positive difference in the lives of others.

~Famous Dave Anderson
Founder of the World's Greatest BBQ Joint!

Start Building Your Success Library of Positive Inspiring Books!

1. Think and Grow Rich, by Napoleon Hill
2. Rich Dad, Poor Dad, by Robert Kiyosaki
3. The World's Greatest Salesman, by Og Mandino
4. Recipes For Success, by Famous Dave Anderson & James Anderson
5. Acres of Diamonds, by Russell Conwell (downloadable free on google)
6. How to Win Friends & Influence People, by Dale Carnegie
7. The Richest Man in Babylon, by George S Clauson
8. The 7 Habits of Highly Effective People, by Stephen R. Covey
9. Secrets of the Millionaire Mind, by T. Harv Eker
10. The Success Principles, by Jack Canfield
11. Maximum Achievement, by Brian Tracy
12. Lessons on Life, by Jim Rohn
13. There's Always A Way, by Tony Little
14. Use Your Head To Get Your Foot In The Door, by Harvey MacKay

Build Your "University On Wheels" Audio Success Library!
Don't ever get into another car without listening to positive inspiring audio books on your car's stereo.

1. The Art of Exceptional Living, by Jim Rohn
2. The New Psychology of Achievement, by Brian Tracy
3. Use Your Head To Get Your Foot In The Door, by Harvey MacKay
4. Live Your Dreams, by Les Brown
5. Celebrate Life, by Leo Buscaglia
6. The Answer, by John Assaraf
7. Expect Miracles, by Joe Vitale
8. It's Your Time, by Joel Osteen
9. Rich Dad, Poor Dad, by Robert Kiyosaki
10. Mentored by A Millionaire, by Steven K. Scott
11. How to Be A Winner, by Zig Ziglar
12. There's Always A Way, by Tony Little

All books, CDs, or DVDs can be found in the Self Improvement Section of your local bookstore or go on line. You can always order my books from my website www.FamousDaveAnderson.com Also check out the number one Personal Development company in the world—www.nightingale.com

THE BUILDER

I saw a gang of men from my home town,
A gang of men tearing a building down,
With a heave and a ho and a yes, yes yell,
They swung a beam and a sidewall fell.

And I went up to the foreman and said, "Are these men skilled?
Like the ones you'd use if you had to build?"
And he laughed and said, "Oh no, no indeed,
The most common labor is all I need...
For I can destroy in a day
What has taken a builder ten years to build."

So I thought to myself as I went on my way...
Which one of these roles am I willing to play?
Am I one who is tearing down
As I carelessly make my way around?

Or am I one whose community will be a little bit better...
Just because I was there?

- Author Unknown

Have Famous Dave Anderson Speak to Your Audience!

A highly sought-after keynote speaker, Famous Dave holds nothing back as he shares his incredible real-life story of overcoming tremendous odds, adversity, and failure to create one of America's best-loved restaurant companies. With passion, energy, and enthusiasm, Dave shares how he overcame his own personal challenges to become America's Rib King. He connects directly to the spirit of every heart in attendance. Dave Anderson is an inspiring speaker and successful entrepreneur whose "Against-All-Odds" story is living proof the American Dream no longer has to be just a dream!

Famous Dave Anderson's most-requested keynotes include:

- **Entrepreneurship:** The Famous Dave's Story—How I Took a Backyard Hobby and Turned it Into a $500 Million Restaurant Empire!

- **Against All Odds**: How to Overcome Life's Adversities and Turn Them Into Your Greatest Opportunities!

- **The Accelerated Changing Marketplace**: Don't Be a Victim of Change—Become the Architect of Your Own Destiny!

- **Sobriety, Freedom, and a New Life**: A Faith-Based Message of Hope and Deliverance From Addictions

In addition to his highly motivating and dynamic keynote presentations, Famous Dave Anderson provides...

- Corporate Coaching for Business Success and Marketing

- Branding Evaluations and Coaching for Businesses

To request Dave as a keynote speaker or to learn more about his personalized coaching programs for businesses, please visit: www.FamousDaveAnderson.com

Have James Speak to Your Audience!

INSPIRING   MOTIVATING   CHALLENGING

James W. Anderson is America's Success Speaker!
To book James for your next conference or event, please contact:
James Anderson Productions
Office: 952.929.1678 or
info@jamesandersonproductions.com

We want to hear from you!

Log onto www.jamesandersonproductions.com and leave me feedback on how this book has inspired you, and receive a FREE MP3 Download of success tips!

Leaders Listen to James!

"After 25 years of listening and learning about personal development, I believed I had learned it all.   I was mistaken. I learned new things because of James about becoming a better manager, father and individual.   James brought the message home with passion and conviction, James was insightful and convincing, I was moved to see such wisdom in a young man.   I have a lot of appreciation to James for helping me take a few more steps up the personal development ladder. "

- Gary Chappell, President/CEO,
Nightingale Conant

Read James W. Anderson's latest books, Yesterday's Wisdom, Today's Success, and Great Results Start With Great Thoughts for Teens

A Special Message from Famous Dave...

I Gratefully Acknowledge

Over the years, I have been amazed at the number of people who have come up to me in my restaurants exclaiming how brilliant I am to have created such a terrific restaurant concept and Famous Dave's is their family's MOST favorite restaurant! I can't help but think back to when I was going through bankruptcy and having a tough time with my drinking—back then I seriously doubted if my dreams would ever become reality. Today, I am very open about the challenges in my life that had to change because overcoming my life's adversities is what makes my story meaningful to the students who read this book. *If I can succeed in college and in life... anyone can succeed!*

I can honestly say today I live a life of gratefulness because of the mentors who came into my life and encouraged me to reach for the stars. I am very thankful to several teachers who made a significant difference in my life. I know I disappointed my parents for the awful grades I got in grade school and high school. Today, I have to thank them for caring enough to make me sit at the kitchen table every night to do my homework. I think I finally made them proud when I received my Master's Degree from Harvard University and they finally had confirmation that their kid wasn't so dumb after all—even though I was 36 years old when I graduated!

I also want to thank my wife, Kathy, for believing in me all these years through the tough times and through the good times. You will never achieve anything worthwhile in life until you have someone who never gives up on you, and while all others doubted me Kathy always encouraged me to hang in there. I'd like to thank my two sons Timothy and James, who inspired me to greater achievements.

I would like to personally acknowledge a terrific young man, Brandon Johnson, who has helped create the LifeSkills Center for Leadership along with myself and my son James Anderson. Brandon's energetic spirit and dedication to building up our nation's greatest resource, students, has been nothing short of spectacular! Other contributors have been my University of Minnesota, Carlson School of Business mentee, Jena Barch, and Kristopher Shelton, a recent graduate of the University of Minnesota, Duluth campus.

I would be remiss if I didn't thank an amazing young lady, who is extremely brilliant: Claire Terrones, my trusted assistant, who has learned how to deal with my attention deficit disorder and keep me on track. Without Claire, I would be staring out the windows not getting anything done, just like in school when my teachers used to get frustrated with me!

I would like to thank my incredible son Tim. Tim taught me patience and to never give up when he showed up with orange hair. I learned that the world wasn't coming to an end and it was only hair! Everyone in life has a need to express themselves in their own way. Some are creative, some are analytical, some are expressive, and some are deep thinkers. The most important lesson I learned from my son is that every child is blessed with their own amazing talents and their own special way of seeing the world. It takes guts to do something that stands out against the norm, but we would never have great thinkers, new innovative creations, new forms of art, or new music if students like my son were not out there pushing the limits to see what is possible!

Finally, I'd like to thank my son James, who has not only been an inspiration while collaborating with me on creating this book but also helped develop our remarkable training programs. James has worked side by side with me throughout the years, as we discovered vital strategies to inspire and motivate college students to achieve success beyond anything they thought possible. This book is the result of ten years of in-the-trenches work with both high school students and college students. There have been many head-scratching moments, but the rewards of seeing the amazing achievements by students that James and I have worked with has been nothing short of incredible.

Dedicated With Humbleness and Appreciation

This book is dedicated to all the amazing teachers who have dedicated their lives inspiring and giving hope to our students. In particular, Dr. Richard St. Germaine, a professor at the University of Wisconsin, Eau Claire Campus, who encouraged me to believe it was possible to get my Master's Degree from Harvard University even though I had lousy grades in high school and I didn't have my undergraduate degree. Dr. St. Germaine influenced me to begin writing, as I always was intrigued by his ability to sit down at a typewriter and just pound away. And today, here I am writing books, even though English was my worst subject!

This book is dedicated to all the incredible parents who continue to see the genius in their children when the rest of the world is scratching their heads wondering if this kid will ever amount to anything. Most of all... this book is dedicated to all the students who have their own dreams for making their mark on mankind. Our students are the hope of our great country and they are tomorrow's leaders as well as great leaders today.

Finally, this book is dedicated to all the employees at Famous Dave's who are either parents with children or students who have jobs at Famous Dave's. I feel extremely grateful to our Chief Executive Officer, Christopher O'Donnell, who in many ways helped make this book possible. I felt if I could share the knowledge that I have gained over the years with the young people within our influence, then they could experience unlimited opportunities and success within their own lives. I believe writing a book that encourages our college-bound students to succeed in school and ultimately in life, could be my greatest gift back to our Famous Dave's team.